MW00809061

HOW AN ENTREPRENEUR CAN LEAD A TEAM SUCCESSFULLY

VALERIE C. RIGGS

© Copyright Valerie C. Riggs, January 2023 - All rights reserved.

The content contained within this book may not be reproduced, duplicated, or transmitted without direct written permission from the author or the publisher.

Under no circumstances will any blame or legal responsibility be held against the publisher, or author, for any damages, reparation, or monetary loss due to the information contained within this book. Either directly or indirectly. You are responsible for your own choices, actions, and results.

Legal Notice:

This book is copyright protected. This book is only for personal use. You cannot amend, distribute, sell, use, quote, or paraphrase any part, or the content within this book, without the consent of the author or publisher.

Disclaimer Notice:

Please note the information contained within this document is for educational and entertainment purposes only. All effort has been executed to present accurate, up-to-date, and reliable, complete information. No warranties of any kind are declared or implied. Readers acknowledge that the author is not engaging in the rendering of legal, financial, medical, or professional advice. The content within this book has been derived from various sources. Please consult a licensed professional before attempting any techniques outlined in this book.

By reading this document, the reader agrees that under no circumstances is the author responsible for any losses, direct or indirect, which are incurred as a result of the use of the information contained within this document, including, but not limited to, errors, omissions, or inaccuracies.

To protect the privacy of certain individuals, names and identifying details have been changed.

Special Note:

I think you will enjoy reading the true stories of entrepreneurs and other leaders who personify the qualities I write about in this book. Their names and business names have been changed to protect their privacy. Likewise, the names of our staff have been changed in the book. That said, my husband and I are using our names and the name of our business with the hope that you'll be inspired by our story.

Table of Contents

Part I. The Foundation of Success

"Alone we can do so little; together we can do so much."

❧Helen Keller❦

Imagine a typical day in your workweek. You might begin the day at your favorite coffee shop, then head to your workplace—a small startup or huge corporation, a manufacturing plant, a university, or even a surf shop. Whatever your work environment, you will likely interact with your immediate circle of co-workers for at least part of the day. At the end of the day, it's off to the grocery store, or if it's been a particularly long day, you might stop for takeout.

What does every aspect of a day like this have in common?

Teams. Small teams are everywhere. Sometimes they are in the background (think of all the work it takes to keep your favorite coffee shop running). Other times, *you* are part of the team. If you are *leading* the team, this book is for you. My goal is for you to be sensational. In this book, I will take you on a journey that my husband and I traveled together, running our business. We went from chaos to absolute joy as we learned what it takes to lead a team step by step. Let's get started!

Chapter 1. Saving the Business

My eyes stung with tears when my husband said to me, "I just can't take it anymore."

We had risked everything to purchase and run our own optometry business and witnessing it on the precipice of failure terrified me.

I was out of town that day on business, relaxing in my hotel room, when I got the phone call from my eye-doctor husband, Kevin.

"Why, what's wrong?" I asked.

"The office has become a nightmare," he said.

I was 500 miles away and couldn't help him. The frustration I felt was unbearable.

"Christine and Sherry aren't speaking to each other, and Suzanne can't seem to stay focused on a task for more than a few minutes. I can't see patients and deal with all of this, too." Christine and Sherry were his opticians; Suzanne, the receptionist.

"They aren't even speaking to each other? That is ridiculous! I'll be home tomorrow," I told him, "We'll deal with it then."

The next day when I arrived at his office, the phones were ringing off the hook, patients were complaining about the glasses Dr. Cole (the seller of the practice) had made for them, and Jane (Dr. Cole's wife, whom we had kept on) was doing people's "color analysis" and discussing the patient's makeup options.

I found Kevin seated in his office with his forehead resting on his desk. He lifted his head and looked at me. I could tell he was on the verge of crying.

"I need her to sell glasses!" he said as we overheard Jane's strange focus with the patient. He sounded desperate.

I hadn't seen him this upset in a long time. He was melting down. It was a shock to me because he had graduated from Optometry College at the University of California, Berkeley, which was no easy feat. I thought he could handle anything.

But when I realized my brilliant husband had no idea how to manage a staff and that his business was falling apart, I jumped in.

From my experience in corporate America and my research, I crafted a team optimization system based on sequential steps. These steps blend and repeat, like the painting of the Golden Gate Bridge. When the Golden Gate Bridge painting crew finishes applying the orange coat to the far end of the famous bridge, they move the whole operation back to the opposite side and begin to paint again. It never stops. That is how these color-coded steps work. Once you reach the Indigo level, you will focus on the Powder Blue level again and refine all your work.

As I implemented my new system, I felt confident that my procedures would work. Still, when they caused us to exceed our already high goals, I knew I was onto something: a new and different method that is easy to follow, effective, and fun.

You can run a brilliant team by following this modern, simple system that any business owner or manager can apply. This method works for start-up businesses, established companies, and for-profit and nonprofit organizations. It even works for families, as a team is similar to a family. This book is a step-by-step, color-coded method clearly laid out for you. Following this guide, a harmonious, happy, and efficient staff quickly becomes a reality. I call the ideal team you will create using this approach an "Indigo team."

As we move through the levels from Powder Blue to Indigo, I'll share my story and the stories of others who are building—and finding great success with—their own Indigo teams.

❧*Even Large Companies Are Made Up of Small Teams*☙

I made a fantastic discovery after creating my color-coded building-block team management system. It turns out that this method can work for managers in huge companies! A close friend's husband, Justin, works for an international defense and technology company. Justin had worked for the company for four years as an engineer when a management position became available. He applied for the job and was excited when he got the promotion.

Justin's job before the promotion had been very hands-on. Every day, he would walk up and down the vast, wide-open floors of the building, examining various innovations and playing with incredible technology while he talked with the engineers. He loved it!

But as he began his management role, Justin had serious doubts about taking his career in this direction. He now sat in his office most of the day handling e-mails; sometimes, he was called into a meeting with other managers. He missed studying the prototypes of cutting-edge technology and discussing them with the innovators.

It looked like it would be a long, grim 16 years until he could retire with full benefits and a pension. He spent endless hours recording the latest stats on his team's performance. Justin felt like prison walls were closing in around him. He dreamed of escaping to Florida and opening a dive shop.

He had a choice. He could wait for his career to conclude (16 years!) or move to Florida and purchase a business.

One evening, a group of friends—including Justin—met for dinner. The group talked and laughed, enjoying catching up with one another. Justin, however, was quiet. He seemed despondent, even. After he told me about his situation at work, I asked, "Why don't you try the color-coded management system I created for entrepreneurs?" Justin raised his eyebrows,

"Entrepreneurs?"

Perhaps Justin's mind was elsewhere (like the dive shop he longed to own), but he said he would look over the information about my method. Could it be something he would utilize with his small team within a giant corporation? Only time would tell.

I didn't hear from Justin for a while. Then one day, I received a message from him. He had taken the Indigo team system step by step, giving each level his full attention. Justin's direct boss appreciated his initiative and supported him along the way.

The result was that through each team level, Justin's daily experience *transformed*, and he enjoyed his job again. His team thrived and even broke some performance records, which upper management noticed. The last time we talked, he had his eye on his boss' job, which he heard might open up soon.

Justin's story shows that not only can the Indigo team method save entrepreneurs' businesses, but it can also save a new manager's career.

Chapter 2. What Is an "Indigo Team"?

An Indigo team is a small group of people committed to a shared mission who work together at a high level of excellence. Everyone gets along *and* achieves company-set goals. If you have more than eight employees, divide your teams into these small units and apply the same principles.

Most entrepreneurs are great at their specialty but could often use more education to manage their personnel. However, you don't need a master's in business administration to lead a successful team. Traditional management methods—such as the annual performance review or working in closed spaces like cubicles instead of open spaces with comfortable seating and lots of light—can be outdated.

Many small business owners pay more attention to their profession, services, and products than their employees. However, it is the employees who make it all happen. Sometimes the most focused, energetic entrepreneur forgets about—or doesn't realize the importance of—keeping his or her eyes on the prize: a happy, fulfilled team who will create great things.

The unpleasant consequences of ignoring a team might include habitual tardiness, dreadful attendance, poor performance, strife with other staff members, negativity, and ultimately high turnover. But with the Indigo team structure, you will find solutions to these challenges!

The concept of an Indigo team results from the years we experienced without one. I watched my husband running his optometry practice. We both knew there had to be a better way to run the business—an approach that was not only financially successful but, as importantly, made the office a welcoming place to be.

Kevin became an optometrist by studying at the University of California at Berkeley for eight years. Unfortunately, during all that time, the professors *never* taught their students how to manage staff. I know it's hard to believe, but Kevin had not received even one hour of management education by the time he graduated.

So, to help him, I used my many years of corporate management experience (with companies including American Airlines, Chevron, and others) to map out how to build the ultimate team. I aspired to create a team that functioned harmoniously. Ultimately, I hoped to establish a new way of working as a team: a group of individuals who would operate so efficiently together that our financial dreams would come true. I also wanted to make a positive difference in all of our employees' lives. So, I worked diligently to clarify an Indigo team's principles and identify the necessary building blocks.

This book spells out our journey and the precise steps to creating a true Indigo team. An Indigo team is a team of harmony, happiness, and efficiency, which, as you can predict, leads to significant profits.

With six colors in the blue color palette leading up to the final and seventh shade, "Indigo," this team-building strategy is a playbook for entrepreneurs—a comprehensive guide to successfully creating and managing a small team.

I've structured the book so that it's easy for readers to come back and start reading from any skill level your team may lack. For instance, perhaps you read this book and master all the Indigo colors except maintaining a solid communication system (the Turquoise level). In that case, you could come back to review the Turquoise level at any time and revisit the concepts so that you're back on track.

With that said, I recommend you give this book a complete read at least once so that you're familiar with all the magic that goes into building your ultimate team. So, let's get started!

৵৵

To become a genuinely Indigo team, you must first undergo a few preluding stages. I've classified them into the following seven levels: Powder Blue, Azure, Turquoise, Cornflower, Cobalt, Amethyst, and Indigo.

Each stage represents the team skill level of "blue/purple" in your small team.

I am using the blue and purple color palettes to symbolize passion, brilliance, and synergy—*the highest potential your team can reach to be of the most value to your business.* The seven stages of the Indigo team make the journey easy for you and help you keep track of your progress. These colors will guide you throughout the process and help you build your successful, happy, money-making dream team.

Powder Blue

At this first step, Powder Blue is focused on defining your mission and putting together a great team. You will clarify the number and types of positions you want to offer. Powder Blue tasks include writing clear and inspiring job descriptions, finding the right people for your team, and training them to start the job.

If you already have a team in place, you will want to determine whether you have the correct job descriptions and the right people executing those jobs.

Azure

In the Azure stage, you will establish your workplace culture. This is the time to focus on fairness, kindness, excellence, and teamwork principles. It's also when you decide on your team's correct salaries, benefits, and schedules to ensure equality.

Turquoise

Turquoise is the stage at which you focus on communication. For example, you may use surveys and active listening techniques and conduct fun staff meetings. The idea is to choose a few of the best lines of communication and use them often to stay in touch with your employees regularly and encourage them to stay in touch with each other.

Cornflower

When you reach the Cornflower stage, you are halfway there! Now is the time to create a brilliant physical space for your team based on comfort, efficiency, and beauty. It's where you'll be doing some of your best work, so it's a good idea to invest in it.

Cobalt

The Cobalt level is about building strong team connections and encouraging team interaction among all members of your company. This is accomplished with team activities and events. The goal is: all team relationships are built on trust, loyalty, respect, kindness, understanding, and shared affirmations.

Amethyst

The Amethyst level is focused on advanced training and mentoring so that your team is equipped with the right skills and is ready to take on the market.

Indigo

The Indigo phase is all about high vibrations. Everyone is responsible for bringing to the team a high level of responsibility, energy, values, and a fantastic attitude. While the business owner (you, or you and your partner/s) sets the tone, equal involvement wins the game—words and actions matter.

In the following chapters, you'll find a step-by-step guide and a cheerleader all in one as you embark on a journey to build your company's Indigo team.

You'll find old ideas revamped into new strategies and entirely new ideas destined to revolutionize team building. We'll work together, weed out bad habits, and learn actionable, proven methods to take your team from Powder Blue to Indigo before you know it.

❧*A Bed and Breakfast Indigo Team*❧

Ten years ago, my friend Marissa and her sister Molly opened a bed and breakfast on the beautiful island of Maui. Their goal was to replace their 9-to-5 jobs with this entrepreneurial venture by the sea.

They purchased a beautiful house with a grassy backyard, just steps from the beach. Almost every room in the house had a picture-perfect view: waves crashing up against lava rocks just yards away. To my friends, it seemed like a gold mine.

But business success is never that easy. Marissa and Molly had no foundation in business; Marissa had been an instructor at the YMCA, and Molly taught dance and physical education at the local high school. So, they ran the business like they ran their own homes, focusing on making their guests feel comfortable.

However, a B&B requires a staff, and the real difficulties started as the sisters began to hire employees. The chef, the housekeeper, the groundskeeper, the reservations desk manager, and the general manager all had to work together to produce happy customers. As you could predict, this didn't happen without a system in place.

When I went to Hawaii to visit them, they were down about what was happening with their business. Their occupancy rate was low. They were getting one-, two-, and three-star reviews and losing money every month. It could not continue this way.

I suggested they try my Indigo team system, and they said

they had nothing to lose. So they jumped into Powder Blue activities and crafted a mission statement and job descriptions. They moved up the building blocks slowly but with determination. As they climbed to higher levels, they were finally breaking even.

One day the sisters looked at their quarterly income statement and were thrilled when they saw a substantial improvement—they were solidly in the black. The same day, an incident happened at the B&B that convinced them they had finally created an Indigo team.

A mother, father, and teenage daughter booked a room in the house. They ordered breakfast in their room before heading out to the beach. The daughter ordered a blueberry scone but ate only half of it, knowing she would enjoy the rest when she returned.

The housekeeper removed the scone from the desk where it sat and threw it into the trash. But then she thought of the mission and wondered if throwing out the half-eaten scone was the best action for the guest. So she went to the pastry chef and asked for a fresh blueberry scone. The chef was happy to help, and when the scone was ready, he called the general manager to take it to the family's room.

When the family came back from the beach, and their

daughter saw a brand new, fresh scone, they were delighted! They knew for sure that the staff truly cared about their experience.

When Marissa and Molly found out this had happened (they saw the 5-star review), they were amazed at how their employees kept the mission of the B&B in mind, communicated with each other, and fulfilled their roles for the greater good. Now that is an Indigo team!

Part II. The Powder Blue Stage: Laying the Foundation

"Talent wins games, but teamwork and intelligence win championships."

❧Michael Jordan☙

Now that you know what an Indigo team is all about, let's lay the foundation for getting there. In the previous chapter, I hinted at how it will feel when your team is at the Indigo stage: *you will be working harmoniously to the team's highest potential to be of the most value to your business.* As you can imagine, this doesn't happen overnight. There will be times when you and your team have made it to a certain level, but things fall apart. There's no shame in that! You'll go back to the step that needs more work, and you and your team will ultimately be stronger for the experience.

Chapter 3. Create a Mission Statement

Unfortunately, it took Kevin and me a few years to get our arms around the situation in our dysfunctional business. I can now see that we started running Kevin's practice prematurely; we launched the practice before establishing *why* we wanted to own this business. This lack of planning led to the staff heading off in many different directions with no cohesive mission. To create this unifying mission for your business, think about why you are in business in the first place. What is your passionate reason for doing what you do? Then write that down, keeping it concise and meaningful. That is your mission statement.

Once Kevin and I established our Grossmont Eye Center mission statement, the staff began pulling in the same direction. (Still, there was plenty more dysfunction to come.) But here was our beginning:

Mission Statement for Grossmont Vision Center Optometry, Dr. Kevin Riggs:

Our mission is to help our patients see their best and look their best by providing the highest technology in vision care, lenses, and frames in an informative and caring environment.

When bringing individuals together to form a team, it is imperative to start by defining your mission. Unless you have a collective vision to work toward, your efforts will be futile. As author Stephen Covey writes in his book *The Seven Habits of Highly Effective People*, you need a map to reach a destination. And if it's the wrong map, no matter how fast you go or how efficient you are, you will get to the wrong place. In other words, speed only helps you when you're headed in the right direction.

A mission statement defines your company's purpose. It helps you articulate and communicate your organization's intentions to employees, customers, and vendors.

To have a focused mission, think about the long run—where you are going, why you're going there, and why it matters. Clarifying these things for yourself also means you define them for your team.

You can't expect your team to dedicate all their time and energy to a cause that benefits only you. The mission also needs to be theirs and the people they serve. It needs to speak to them individually and inspire them to act. The collective dedication toward one common goal will also build a strong workplace culture, which—as you will see in the coming chapters—will gradually turn your team from Powder Blue to Azure.

Since mission statements usually define a long-run purpose and focus, you won't need to alter them over time.

Let's consider a few examples.

Patagonia

Build the best product, cause no unnecessary harm, and use business to inspire and implement solutions to the environmental crisis.

American Express

We work hard every day to make American Express the world's most respected service brand.

IKEA

To create a better everyday life for many people.

You have probably noticed that these mission statements inspire a sense of purpose. Imagine working for a company with a mission like one of these. You would know exactly where the company leadership intends to go and why you are going there.

That's the trick to unifying individuals toward one common end goal (or series of goals): it gives them a reason to come to work.

In Powder Blue (our stage one), you will learn exactly how to do this.

Creating an Inspiring Mission Statement

Have you ever come across a business and wondered what they do and why they do it? What's their story? What's their purpose?

To accelerate the world's transition to sustainable energy.

That is Tesla's mission statement.

The message is simple. It concisely explains to customers and employees what the company hopes to achieve. However, some might say it's more of a vision than a mission. Mission statements should also focus on the present and what you can do *today* to move closer to your goal. A mission statement should inspire action and perhaps even a sense of urgency.

For instance, insurance company Aflac's mission statement is:

To combine aggressive strategic marketing with quality products and services at competitive prices to provide the best insurance value for consumers.

It tells customers that they value quality products and services at competitive prices. But for employees, it lays out a series of steps to ensure they follow the company's mission. For instance, *they want to actively work toward aggressive strategic marketing, quality products and services, competitive prices, and the best insurance value for consumers.* The mission statement spells these actions out clearly.

While this mission statement doesn't provide context for its bigger vision and isn't too inspirational, it provides a solid direction. The key to a brilliant mission statement is learning to balance both a passionate vision and the actions required to achieve that vision.

Finding the Balance Between Inspiration and Action

The best mission statement balances an aspirational promise and an actionable plan. It spells out a vision for your team and clarifies the path of action to achieve this vision.

The first part may say, *We strive to become an industry leader*

But the second part ought to go like this: *by offering high-quality products and working hard to ensure good service.*

Neither of those statements would stand out on its own, but when you combine them, you will have a powerful mission statement!

The Key Elements of a Mission Statement

There are some essential elements that you can add to create a compelling mission for your business. First, remember that your mission is a declaration of what you think gives your brand purpose. So, in essence, it's meant to guide your team's actions and attract the right customers.

Here are four key elements for creating your mission statement:

Value. What is the *value* of the business to both customers and employees?

Inspiration. Why would people *want* to work for your company?

Achievability. Are your dreams reasonable and *achievable*?

Specificity. How does your mission tie to your *specific* niche or industry?

Let's consider another example. The brand Honest Tea uses a phrase to add value and specificity to its mission statement:

To create and promote great-tasting, healthier, organic beverages.

Then, to add inspiration, Honest Tea also states:

To grow our business with the same honesty and integrity we use to craft our products.

The Dos and Don'ts of a Great Mission Statement

The Dos:

- Keep it brief. Use only a few sentences to sum up the company's mission.

- Think long-term. Your mission is an investment in your organization's future, so make sure that it is broad enough to reflect your long-term goals.

- Find out what your employees think of the mission statement. It's a tool designed for them, so get their opinion. Ask if there is anything that they dislike about it and how they would improve it.

The Don'ts:

- Don't write an essay. Nobody is going to remember long prose. That's not the purpose of this brand-building tool. Instead, you want the mission statement to act as a signal of the brand, which means it must be short, sweet, and memorable.

- Don't limit it too much! *We are the best organic*

and healthy juice shop in Los Angeles. What if you decide to expand to other cities? What if your business takes off, and you add smoothies, muffins, or other healthy items to the menu?

- Having said that, if the need does arise, don't be afraid to change it! Things constantly evolve in the business world. If your mission statement no longer represents the company, it's probably time for a rewrite.

❧ *A Mission Statement Made the Difference* ❧

My friend Claire had loved coffee since her first latte; she was only 10 years old when her grandma made it for her. By the time Claire was 18, she knew she wanted to run a coffee shop. So she majored in business in college, and after graduation, she opened her café.

Even though she focused on the highest quality coffee available to serve her customers and was a stickler for customer service, her business failed to flourish. She had a high employee turnover rate. Also, her customers enjoyed her offerings but didn't seem passionate about her products.

Claire knew I had a business background, so she asked me for help.

I started evaluating her company at the Powder Blue level. The first thing I asked to see was her mission statement. As soon as I read it, I knew she had a fundamental problem.

It read, "To serve our customers the finest coffee drinks as quickly as possible." It was flat and uninspiring. No wonder it had never set her team or her customers on fire!

I showed her Starbucks' mission statement:

"To inspire and nurture the human spirit—one person, one cup, and one neighborhood at a time."

Claire immediately grasped the difference. "I was thinking too small," she said.

She thought about why she loved having a coffee shop and what she dreamed of accomplishing. She posted her new mission statement as a large, beautiful sign behind her counter. It read:

"To delight and comfort our customers by professionally serving delicious coffee drinks and high-quality baked goods in a positive, inspiring environment."

Claire talked about her new mission statement to everyone around her. Customers and employees responded to her vision. The improved mission statement even increased Claire's own energy and commitment! And her strategy paid off. It didn't happen overnight, but eventually, her financials looked better and better.

Now let's figure out how your team is going to look.

Chapter 4. How Many Employees Do You Need?

You now know precisely why you are in business and have written an inspiring and powerful mission statement. You are ready to share it with your current or new staff.

But then you realize that achieving your mission with a staff can get expensive. You must plan, keep track of, and efficiently manage your labor costs.

It can help to determine how many employees you need, why you need each, and how much it will cost to keep him or her. I refer to your employees as "Actors" because it sheds light on how significant each employee's role is in making your mission a reality. Like actors in a play, there is an exact correct number to fulfill the roles.

The Art of Delegation

When entrepreneurs start a firm, it's like our baby, so our reluctance to trust others with its safety and progress is more than understandable. If you have watched the television sitcom "Friends," you will know what I mean when I say that it triggers the "Monica" in many of us. We want to do everything ourselves and ensure everything is perfect and in line and that we are the best in the market. Those are all noble aspirations, but we cannot pull them off alone. Even the best actor in a play will get exhausted if he tries to play every role himself.

A business is, after all, made up of people. So even in a small practice, you will need people with different skills. Perhaps you will hire people with skills you don't have—the best accountant or customer service rep. Sometimes small businesses fail because the entrepreneur overestimates her abilities (or the abilities of her partners or staff). For example, money runs out because there is no one in the finance department who diligently oversees monthly expenses, budgets, and costs. Likewise, customer retention falters because there is no one answering customer queries and helping troubleshoot their problems. I'm sure you see the challenge.

So, besides writing a mission statement, one of the first steps to crafting your Powder Blue team is delegating responsibilities. Next, you will figure out what kind of employees you need and how many you need to complete your team.

Here are some questions you can ask yourself.

- What skills would I like each team member to have so that each will be valuable to my business?

- Where would I find people who possess these skills?

- Is there a specific educational level or qualifications the candidate must have to be part of my team?

- What tests would I like them to pass, or what questions would I want to ask them?

- What personality characteristics do I want my new hires to have?

Nailing down the answers to these questions is crucial to success as we continue our Indigo team journey. Remember, this Indigo method is a build-up; we become sharper, brighter, and savvier with each color level and chapter.

Now that you have figured out *what kind* of actors you need for your play to be a hit on Broadway, let's figure out exactly how many actors you will need. It would help if you calculated your staffing needs.

The Actors in the Play: How Many Team Members Do You Require?

To figure out how many employees you need, you can use a formula like this:

Production units anticipated x

Production time required per unit ÷

(Scheduled time per employee - Forecast of non-productive employee time per employee)

= People needed full time

It is not complicated. Here is an example of how it works. Imagine you own a cake shop. We will take it step by step to determine how many bakers you need.

Production units anticipated

Finding out how many people you need on your team to

realistically meet your production or revenue goals will depend on your business demand.

How many customers do you currently have if you have purchased an existing business? How many do you expect to have? If you have opened a business cold, what number of customers do you believe is realistic from studying similar businesses? You will want to do market research and use your own experience and intuition. In other words, how many cakes will you bake in a day?

In our bakery example, we anticipate requests for 35 cakes a day.

Production time required

Next, you need to know how long it takes one person to bake one cake. Say it takes one hour.

Scheduled hours per employee

Then decide on the hours you will assign your staff to work each day. For example, the standard workday here in the United States is 8 hours.

Forecast of non-productive employee time per employee

No employee can work to meet customer demand 100% of the time. You will decide how much time an employee will be in production mode. If the person is at work 8 hours a day, you might want to subtract .2 hours for meetings, .3 hours for breaks, and .5 hours for personal time (illness, vacation, attending her child's play, etc.) That means, on average, your employee would put in 7 hours a day of pure, productive time.

The answer

So here are the numbers we need for our bakery:

Production Units Anticipated = 35 cakes a day

Production Time Required for Each Unit = 1 hour per cake

Total Production Time Required = 35 hours per day

Scheduled Time per Employee = 8 hours a day

Forecast of Non-Productive Employee Time per Employee = 1 hour a day

Productive Time per Employee = 7 hours a day

Running these numbers through our formula:

Thirty-five cakes a day x 1 hour = 35 hours of production needed per day ÷ (8 hours a day per employee − 1 hour for non-productive time) = the number of bakers necessary to work each day.

So:

35 hours of production time needed per day ÷ 7 hours of productive time per employee per day = five bakers required to work each day

The answer is:

People Needed Full Time = 5

If your business is seasonal, you can simply adjust the number each season and rerun the formula.

Believe me; if I can do this, you can do this. Math is not my most vital subject. Find the number of team members you need.

Clarifying Job Descriptions

We picked up the book *From Good to Great* by Jim Collins early in developing our business. As a result, we became familiar with the concept of identifying the correct "seats on the bus" or job positions needed to run our business.

You have already figured out how many actors you need. Now, examine what each of their roles should be. Develop clear job descriptions for each role (or for each seat on the bus). Clear job descriptions avoid problems that sound like this:

"Who is responsible for dusting the shelves during the week to fight all this dust?" (You may think it's only dust. We provide eye care, so the office must be immaculate.)

"Oh, we all do," answered the head optician.

Then, when Kevin notices the shelves are dusty by Thursday, he asks again, "Whose job is it again to dust the shelves? These don't look great."

Christine says, "Oh, I thought Shelley would do it."

Shelley says, "I thought Christine would do it."

We learned that if *everyone* is responsible for a task, *no one* does it.

Without clear, precise job descriptions, this scenario can

happen over and over in all business areas. Who calls the patient and tells her that her glasses are ready? Who verifies a patient's insurance coverage? A hundred tasks like these must be assigned to the right person.

Thus, Kevin wrote detailed job descriptions, and each of us gained clarity about who was responsible for each detail necessary to keep the business running smoothly.

It is now time to do this for your business. Returning to our bakery example, we determined that we would need five bakers daily to meet customer demand. But what about taking the orders, delivering the cakes, ordering ingredients, and maintaining the equipment? Think about how many total roles you need to complete your team and begin writing simple job descriptions that list the job duties of each team member. Once you figure out all the parts you need and have written clear job descriptions, you have the foundation for your hiring process.

❧ *A Surf Shop Hits Some Waves* ❧

When Porter's trust fund finally landed in his bank account, he knew exactly what he wanted to do. He had drawn up the plans for his surf shop on cocktail napkins at the local biker bar called The Kraken. Porter made a habit of going to happy hour, ordering a $3 beer, and planning how to launch the business of his dreams. He saved every planning napkin, even from the time the afternoon bartender would serve him at age 14. Thanks to his grandfather's bequest, the day had come when he could take action.

Due to some good luck (and maybe a bit of family influence with the City Council), Porter signed a lease on a perfect-sized place just blocks from the beach. He ordered all the inventory and then put his efforts into hiring staff. How big should the staff be? Consulting his sometimes-blurry cocktail napkins, he saw that he had originally planned on hiring four employees.

He diligently hired these staff members, trained them, and felt confident all would be well on opening day.

As the days and weeks rolled on with his brand-new business, staffing became quite a balancing act. He had opened his doors during the peak of the summer surfing season (July in San Diego). From 10 a.m. to 5 p.m., he was swamped with various customers—tourists heading to the beach, people in town for horse races, guests from the hotel across the street, and locals needing beach supplies. His staff of four was completely overwhelmed, and the situation began to result in some poor online reviews.

Porter quickly went back into hiring mode and hired three more employees. The rest of the summer went smoothly, and his reviews improved.

Then fall came.

Children were back in school, the horse racing season had ended, vacations were over, and his surf shop became deafeningly quiet—except for the noise coming from his seven rambunctious, youthful employees who passed the time by skateboarding outside the shop, talking to their girlfriends on the phone, and texting party plans to their friends.

Porter felt nervous as he saw the daily sales figures drop and his payroll stay the same. He knew he had to do something. He gathered his team together. He asked if there were any volunteers who would be willing to cut their hours to part-time through the winter and come back full-time in the summer. That solution worked well for two of them, who were students. Another employee told him he had been thinking about backpacking through Europe over the fall and winter and that he could check in before summer to be rehired.

Porter felt great relief over being able to cut the payroll

immediately and was happy with the plan to increase staffing again the following summer.

All these years later, he admits that seasonal staffing is still a big balancing act. But with experience, he has made it work, and his dream of a successful surf shop has come true.

Chapter 5. The Hiring Plan

You are making significant headway in building a fantastic team! You have a compelling mission statement. You have figured out how many employees you need to hire and what will make up each employee's job description.

Now you must find the *right* people. Remember that taking the time to find the right people at this stage is fundamental. So, let's take it slow.

There is a new, modern way of hiring. You no longer ask every applicant to meet with you face-to-face right off the bat. Instead, save that as the last step when you have already vetted them. This process is simple, straightforward, and produces terrific results!

Where can you find these incredible people with the skills, values, and character traits you are looking for? How can you attract them, and where should you even look? Let's begin at the beginning.

Recruiting the Right Talent

Usually, your intuition will tell you how valuable a person

might be as an addition to your staff. But there are some things to remember when building your dream team. One is ensuring that you hire professionals with the necessary specializations and skills, fulfilling your needs as described by each job description.

Crafting the Best Online Job Posting

The first thing you will want to do is write a job posting. It is the first glimpse that potential employees get of your business. It clearly shows what you are looking for and what you have to offer. What skills do you require the candidates to have for each position? Examine the job descriptions you wrote in Chapter 4 to help with this process.

An excellent job posting can make a difference in attracting the talent you desire.

You should ensure that your job postings are accurate. You must meet jobseekers' expectations to ensure that your team members stick around and stay committed. It is wise to avoid over-promising or over-compensating in your job postings. Instead, be honest, realistic, and precise. Because while you may attract great workers at the start, what are the chances that they'll stay around once they find out your job posting misled them? People also need to know the expectations of the role and whether they have the required skills, interests, and expertise for your job opening.

Next, stick to what's most relevant. Remember that candidates usually skim through many job postings and won't bother to read entire essays! So, leave some things for the interview day and target people from as many areas as possible for applications. You never know who might surprise you! The hiring and screening process can be long and tedious if you don't have the right plan. Follow the method below for the best results and the fewest headaches!

Writing excellent job postings is the first part of talent acquisition.

The Hiring Steps

Look for your new team members in many places

To make sure your job posting is powerful and sure to attract the best candidates, include these seven items:

1. Clear layout: Include bullet points and lists for easy reading

2. Job title

3. Job description

4. Job requirements

5. Clear how-to-apply instructions

6. Company name and logo

7. Company overview

Now that you have perfected your job posting, publish it on your favorite recruiting sites (Craigslist, Indeed, LinkedIn, etc.). You can also post on a physical job or community boards wherever you think appropriate (Starbucks, community centers, churches, etc.).

Another great way to find the right people is through connections and networks. No matter who you are, you probably know some people who know others—and just like that, you'll find *your* people. The trick is to get the word out; you never know which acquaintance may surprise you.

Simplify the application process

Candidates typically don't want to participate in long and exhausting application processes. When it comes to application forms, they may often fill them out on mobile phones. They expect you'll read their resumes and ask for other related information in the remaining fields. Leave the rest for the interviews! Don't discourage people at the first stage of the process.

And, of course, it always helps to use an optimized, mobile-friendly application process. Here are the best ones, according to Calendly:

1. Indeed

2. LinkedIn Recruiter

3. Textrecruit

4. Calendly

5. Zip Recruiter

6. Monster

7. Homebase

8. Workable

9. Shapr

Wait for five to seven days to accumulate applications. You are looking for about a dozen potential candidates to begin the hiring process.

Study the applications

Once you have a dozen or so applications, take a good look. Take time to analyze the qualifications of the applicants. Sometimes, talent lurks where nobody looks.

After reviewing each online application carefully, separate it into "Interested" and "Not Interested" groups.

Interview your candidates

Contact each applicant in the "Interested" category to schedule a phone call or Zoom (or another online live-streaming platform) interview.

I suggest following this structured interview process.

Use structured interview questions

A meta-analysis of how thoroughly various assessments predict job performance found that unstructured interviews explain only 14% of employee performance. Structured interviews can predict up to 26% of employee performance (McDaniel et al. 1994). In a structured interview, you ask all candidates the same questions and use clear criteria to assess their responses. As a result, you have treated everyone fairly, used the same standards, and can avoid inconsistencies. Then, all you need to do is define a set of questions you would like the candidates to answer and review and compare the results.

After completing all these live-streaming interviews, again sort the candidates into "Interested" and "Not Interested" categories.

Contact those in the "interested" group and schedule in-person interviews.

Conduct an in-person interview with these remaining candidates and decide which person is best for each job description.

Inform all the candidates of your decision.

Keep candidates engaged

Most managers are unaware of a brilliant strategy to keep candidates engaged throughout the hiring process. It not only avoids walk-aways but also makes the entire process more efficient. You can even use hiring tools like email automation to ensure people stay in the loop about updates.

All you do is create one email template and adjust it slightly to let candidates know about each process step. Then, with a few clicks, you can keep them connected to updates, which can prevent dropouts that are due to a lack of communication. Retaining as many candidates as possible throughout the hiring process is essential.

Congratulations, you've found your people! But just because you've done a thorough and professional job in hiring and your new employees have clear job descriptions, it does not mean they have the skills to do the job well. It's time for training!

A Nut Butter Company's Modern Approach to Hiring

Hailey, a close friend of a close friend, started her nut butter product line part-time while she was still in college. She rented a commercial kitchen and began making the highest quality pure organic nut butter on the market. Hailey finished college and then worked nearly endless hours on her nut butter business. She expected it to be a success, but when it happened, she felt overwhelmed. Hailey couldn't sleep at night because she could no longer keep up with the online orders, no matter how long and hard she worked.

The certainty that she would have to hire employees finally sunk in. When Hailey had envisioned her future business, she had always pictured doing it alone. The hassle, expense, and extra work of hiring a staff made her dread the entire process.

Luckily, she decided to change her mindset to one of gratitude. Here she was, very successful, able to buy a beautiful home in a coastal neighborhood in California. Hailey became determined to increase the momentum of her success by hiring the best people available. But she didn't want to do it traditionally.

She started by asking everyone she knew—clients, staff, vendors, family, and friends—if they knew anyone who would be interested in a job with her. It surprised her how many candidates this brought her! She was able to skip fishing for potential hires via online platforms.

Then Hailey scheduled online interviews with all the candidates whom people recommended to her. But instead of asking the same old interview questions like "Why should I hire you?" or "Where do you see yourself a year from now?" or "What are your greatest strengths and greatest weaknesses?" She used her creativity and came up with some questions she thought would serve her better.

She didn't want to ask questions that made the interviewee uncomfortable, but she did want to have some fun with them and get to know them better, so she came up with a unique method.

Hailey first asked the candidate an Ice Breaker question like, "If you were going to be stuck on a deserted island (and had all the food, water, and shelter you needed), what three personal items would you bring?" or "If you could go to any country (that you haven't been to) where would you go and why?"

Then she would inquire about the candidate's feelings toward work and the food industry. She asked, "Tell me about a time when you were part of a fun team," and "How did you balance productivity and fun with your co-workers?" Hailey felt like this gave her an insight into how potential employees would fit into the company culture she intended to create.

After she asked 10 to 12 unique, non-traditional questions

of the interviewee, Hailey felt like she had a good handle on who the person was. She stopped dreading the hiring process because she didn't have to ask the old, tired interview questions and could use her creativity and curiosity to determine if an applicant was a match for her company.

She hired brilliant, wonderful people with this method and, since this experience, has never resisted the hiring process.

Chapter 6. The Training Plan

The next big shake-up at Grossmont Vision Center Optometry came about when it was time to ensure each current staff member knew how to perform every item on her job description. Sounds easy, right?

Some employees held over from the business purchase liked to hide what they were doing to retain job security. So, when we wanted to document exactly how the business runs, the process of figuring out who did what, when, and how was like discovering classified government secrets.

These inquiries, along with more time observing the skills of the current employees, led to some firings and our first new hires since purchasing the business. In addition, it led to hours of hands-on training related to job descriptions.

It was a painstakingly slow process while we monitored, clarified, and documented each aspect of every job. It took so much patience! There were times when I thought it just couldn't be done. I thought, "Not all companies do this," and that's true. But we didn't want to experience the average employee turnover rate. We wanted our bottom line and our employees' happiness to be far better than average. Line item by line item, our team members learned their jobs daily, and we documented everything in a digital operation manual.

Think about your training plan. You can begin before you go through the hiring process or while going through it. Developing a plan for your basic training program at this stage is smart. It will allow you to gather and arrange the necessary resources and anticipate the time you may need to train your team. Remember that the more organized you are, the fewer chances of failure or potential problems.

Remember that this is just "basic training." More advanced training emphasizing specialization, where a trainer teaches finely honed skills, leads to meeting ambitious goals. This advanced type of education will occur when we reach the Amethyst level. The purpose of the training at the Powder Blue level is to get your team operational.

I've developed a four-step process to help you implement a practical, first-step in-house training program for your current and future team.

The Training Steps

Step 1. Determine your training needs

First, ask yourself what you need your employees to do. What skills would you like them to develop to bring the most value to your company? What hard skills (like entering an order into your software or following a particular procedure) or soft skills (like handling an upset patient) do you want to teach them? Determining the goals for your basic training program ensures that you devise the appropriate content, methods, and materials to get your team up and running. If you have clarity about your learning objectives, your training program has a good chance of success.

Step 2. Share essential instructions before Day One

At the Powder Blue level, all the training is new. Think back to your first day at your job. You were probably nervous—unsure where to park, what to wear, when to show up, who to talk to, or where to eat. So, engaging your new hires before Day One can go a long way in gaining their trust.

According to the Aberdeen Group, 83% of the highest-performing organizations began onboarding the new hire before the new hire's first day. So, instead of letting your trainees flounder on that first morning, I suggest sending an email before they ever show up. You may consider covering the:

- Location and start time of the training

- Instructions for parking

- A quick overview of what their trainer will cover on the first day

- Tools that will be available to them, such as laptops or headphones

- Your contact information so that they can easily communicate with you

- Office dress code

- Information about nearby coffee or lunch places

- A schedule to follow, including breaks, meals, meetings, or hands-on training

As you make it an easy experience right from the start, you'll reduce stress for your new hires, which will help them get off to a great start.

Step 3. Develop and implement your training program

Once you've figured out your learning outcomes and goals,

it's time to research. For example, what resources does your organization have that you could allocate to its training program? What is your training budget? Again, it is an area that pays off when you invest correctly.

Once you have determined the resources for your training program, you can plan and build out its content. Will the training be conducted in a classroom setting, in person, or online? Or will you use a workshop to get everyone participating in hands-on exercises? Be creative. There are many exciting ways to teach adults hard (technical) and soft (people) skills. Give people the proper education and experience, and their confidence will soar.

Set up your program module by module and specify how you will execute the training. For example, in our pretend bakery, we would have:

Module 1: How to Bake a Cake. It would be delivered in a hands-on workshop in our commercial kitchen with a printed recipe from our pastry chef.

Module 2: How to Deliver a Cake. This education would be

presented via a video showing the driver delivering cakes and discussing company policies.

Module 3: Our Customer Service Policy presented in a Zoom call by the owner.

And so on.

Once you have your training program in outline form, you can turn it into a full curriculum by filling in all the details. Run it by some trusted others, tweak it, and move sections around until it is just right.

Organize your training materials to match your curriculum. Install Zoom apps on devices, get Zoom links ready to share, and print out or share manuals, hand-outs, PowerPoint slides, and workbooks. All training materials need to be ready on Day One.

Step 4. Plan to measure results

Next, determine how you gauge whether your employees have learned your training material. For example, you can tell how well the employee absorbs the material by observing how well he is doing his job. This way, you establish methods to track whether the training you have designed is practical or not.

If you see that a trainee has not fully absorbed your material, have him or her repeat modules if necessary. Then you can decide if he or she has the skills for the job. Unfortunately, if an individual cannot grasp the basics of the job you have hired him for, the next step is to let him go.

❧ *Training for the Cat Café* ❧

My friend Isabella had a unique vision for a business after college. Izzy (the name she goes by) knew she wanted to run a café that made delicious espresso drinks and homemade cold brew coffee. Plus, she wanted to feature gourmet pastries made by local pastry chefs. But here is what made Izzy's idea so different: she wanted to run a cat fostering facility and adoption center attached to the café. While sipping their coffee, customers could enjoy the cats in the "cat lounge." Izzy was passionate about putting the people in her community together with cats that needed a loving home, and she was certain this would result in many adoptions. She was right.

But with such a unique business plan, her training needs

for her employees were quite complicated. She would need to find and train people with skills in preparing food and beverages *and* caring for felines—two entirely different skill sets.

In her hiring process, she ensured the candidates had interest and experience in both fields. Then she chose the ones who seemed to have the most compassion for the cats.

At first, Izzy felt overwhelmed at the thought of training her employees to do varied tasks, from making a beautifully crafted coffee drink to cleaning the litter boxes and refreshing the cats' food and water. For one thing, sanitary practices and cleanliness had to come first since she was mixing food and animals. How was she going to ensure that her staff took this as seriously as she did, plus master all the cat care and food preparation skills?

I spoke to her briefly at a beach party as she faced this daunting task. After we discussed best practices for training employees, I heard from a mutual friend that Izzy had developed and executed a well-organized and original (like everything Izzy did) staff training program.

When I happened to run into her several months later at our local farmer's market, I asked her how the staff training went. She told me it was a big success, that business was going well, and that her customers raved about her café offerings and had adopted many of her fostered cats.

Izzy wrote every training module herself and allowed plenty of time for each module's execution. Always the innovator, she created a points system woven into the sessions. A trainee could gain or lose points during a simulated scenario based on the expectations laid out in the training module. For example, if the new hire remembered to wash her hands after tending to one of the cats, she gained 10 points. Izzy offered a prize to the person who finished the program with the most points.

Izzy's training program had everything a training program should have. She developed it to be highly organized, creative, and effective. Now years later, her café is thriving and is a local legend among food and animal lovers.

Chapter 7. Gentle Firing

Once the shock wore off over the reality that the Grossmont Vision Center staff was problematic, we jumped into solution mode. It took us a minute because we had paid a substantial amount for this business, and we believed that a functional team was part of the deal!

But it became evident that Mrs. Cole, the former head doctor's wife, had to go. She had a total sense of ownership over the business because she and her husband had owned it for 30 years. So, directing or managing her was impossible. She was going to do as she had always done and do whatever she wanted. We knew that our first firing had to happen.

With much anxiety and pain, we let Mrs. Cole go. And then, the business finally seemed under our management. But now we had to manage!

You will make a team of people who should fit together like pieces of a puzzle. As you continue your journey to building an Indigo team, you'll find the right people to be part of it. What about when a staff member (one you have hired or inherited) doesn't work out? You *must* let him or her go, or an Indigo team is impossible. And you will want to do it right away before the environment becomes toxic. Every team member must have the right skills *and* the right attitude.

Establish your Powder Blue team (level 1) and lay the foundation for your Azure team (level 2). At this point, you want team members who fit your mission statement and job criteria. They should also be willing to adopt your team culture. But what do you do if things with a team member go south? How do you fire someone without offending him if he is not engaged in your mission, isn't up to par, or you can tell doesn't want to be there? Is there even such a thing? We'll find all that and more in this chapter.

Master the Art of (Almost) Pain-Free Firing

Look, firing employees is not pleasant for anyone. However, letting an employee go will always be the most challenging part of your job. And yes, you are doing your best to ensure that your Indigo team is top-notch, using a quality hiring process. Needing to fire someone won't often happen unless you have purchased a business with a staff already chosen by someone else. However, if I've learned anything from my husband's clinic, it's that things happen. And sometimes, problems surface from places you least expect.

Letting people go doesn't have to be a harrowing experience. By addressing some fundamental issues at the roots of your firm, you can ensure that there is usually no need to fire anyone you hire. If you do, it can happen smoothly. It should be a relatively pain-free experience for everyone. Follow these steps, and it will all be okay.

Step 1. Stay up to date on job performance reviews

It is easiest for everyone to let someone go if you fire him or her on job performance issues. However, suppose you have not documented or discussed those issues with the employee along the way. Now your communication with your employee becomes awkward. We'll discuss how to conduct job performance reviews effectively when we get to the Turquoise team.

Don't wait a year to let the staff know how they are doing! That is an old-fashioned management method. It is much better to check in with each team member on performance at least once a month. Then, if you decide that someone must go, you can go over monthly reviews and say, "I'm going to have to let you go because of these ongoing issues." Clean and swift, understandable, and straightforward.

Step 2. You can fire immediately for a breach of company policy

We had to do an unexpected firing once when we discovered that one of our employees was treating one of our other employees disrespectfully. The disrespected employee let us know what was happening. We verified the facts, listened to both sides, then let the offending employee go immediately.

Every employee signs a standard Employee Agreement, so you will want to let them go when they break this agreement. However, once an employee breaches a policy, do not let the toxicity and dysfunctionality spread. It is a "pack up, hand over your keys" type of situation, which you will handle with grace and compassion.

Step 3. Make it as undramatic as possible

When you need to let someone go, include a third party in the meeting—a business partner, a manager, or a trusted employee. Having a witness will help you avoid legal issues. Go into your office with your employee and your chosen other and close the door. It is also best to handle the termination when all the other team members have left for the day. It is much less humiliating for the fired employee to pack his or her belongings without the other team members witnessing this. And let's be realistic—crying is a possibility. Better to have no one around if this occurs. Stay calm, kind, and professional; it will be over soon.

A Bridal Shop Firing

Julianne, a friend's daughter, surprised her family with the news that she had purchased a David's Bridal franchise. Julianne was a beautiful, vivacious blonde who had just turned thirty. She had been working for the state government in a tedious, dead-end job and had dreamed about and saved up for this radical career change. Her parents were shocked, her husband was shocked, and they tried to talk her out of it, but it was too late; she had already signed the papers.

Running the franchise and making a profit came easy to Julianne, but firing an employee seemed to her like an impossible task. Although she carefully hired her staff, one of her sales agents was not working out.

The problem was that this team member, Rebecca, had a way of insulting the brides and losing sales. She would say things like, "With your large size, we're going to need a slimming silhouette," or "With your flat chest, I don't think this halter style will work."

Julianne had trained her staff on how to speak to a customer respectfully, but Rebecca could not seem to use the correct script. Julianne worked with Rebecca repeatedly but then overheard Rebecca again speaking bluntly to a bride. Finally, Julianne accepted that Rebecca was not a fit for her company; Julianne knew she would have to fire Rebecca. She dreaded it.

That morning, Julianne was nervous. She had never fired anyone. She gathered her courage and waited until Rebecca finished with a client.

Then she heard Rebecca say to her client, "With such short hair, you will need an extra feminine dress." Julianne cringed.

She immediately asked another employee to handle Rebecca's customer and waved Rebecca into her office.

"Haven't I asked you a dozen times not to refer to the bride's physical features?" Julianne asked Rebecca.

"Yes, but I can help them better if I do!" Rebecca argued.

"Rebecca, I'm going to have to let you go. Please gather up your belongings and turn in your key. I am sorry it didn't work out." Julianne was shaking, and her palms were sweating. She could see the shock on Rebecca's face. Then the tears in her eyes. But Julianne remained professional even though she felt like Jell-o.

When Rebecca finally said her goodbyes to the rest of the staff, gathered up her stuff, and relinquished her key, Julianne felt a great sense of relief. Sometimes the most difficult things are also the most needed. For her customers and her team, Julianne had done the right thing.

Now you have yourself a solid Powder Blue team! You have an incredible mission statement; you have identified the number of employees you need and what each job position entails with detailed job descriptions. You have hired the right people and let people who do not match your criteria go. Your training program has helped every staff member on the team know how to perform his or her job. Time to level up to Azure, where we establish our company culture!

Key Takeaways

Here is what you want to do to solidify your team at the Powder Blue level:

- Create a remarkable, inspiring mission statement.

- Determine the precise number of positions (parts in the play or seats on the bus) you need to achieve your mission.

- Create clear job descriptions that you have assigned to each team member.

- Create job postings describing what you are looking for in a new hire and what you have to offer.

- Follow a modern, professional hiring process that utilizes the internet to efficiently hire the most qualified candidates.

- Plan out a basic training program to prepare for your future team.

- Once your team is in place, conduct your basic training program to educate your staff on their job descriptions.

- Optimize your firing process by avoiding any unnecessary drama or negativity.

- Put effort into this Powder Blue team level to create a solid foundation. The actions in this chapter increase the value of your business and prepare the way for successful team building.

Part III. The Azure Team: Company Culture

"Being kind, thoughtful, and empathetic are essential leadership skills that can cascade through a team, changing the workplace culture."

&⯈Valerie C. Riggs⯇&

Imagine a set of building blocks that look like this: the base is powder blue, the next level is azure, and so on until you reach the top, indigo. That's how we designed our team levels. It's not that we leave behind the tenets of one level to move to the next; instead, we build and keep building. When we need to do so, we might go back to a previous, more fundamental level to shore up our strengths. It's a continuous process.

Witnessing the exciting changes as we created our "base" (our Powder Blue team), Kevin and I knew we had to keep building. We wanted to create a principle-bound and emotionally healthy workplace. The next level would be the Azure level of our team, focused on core values. Fairness, kindness, excellence, teamwork, and good health are all part of the company culture that contributes to this level.

Chapter 8. Establishing the Team Culture

Just as the foundation of a building keeps it solid, and the roots of a tree keep it alive, the support you build for your team will determine everything about your firm's future and success. This support starts with your core values, priorities, and belief systems.

Core Team Values Help You Win

Healthy workplace culture is essential to building a brilliant team. It will become easier to work together as you focus on shared values and goals, including your mission statement. You will effortlessly collaborate because everyone will have the same results in mind.

> A reporter asked San Diego Padres pitcher Pierce Johnson why he thought the Padres had such success early in the 2021 season. He replied, "We mesh together."
>
> "Yes, I can see that. But *why* do you mesh so well?" the sports reporter asked.

Pierce replied simply, "Because we are all playing the same game."

The players, coaches, and staff align with what they are doing (the mission) and how they do it (their values).

We have already emphasized the mission. And now, by prioritizing *team values*, team members can avoid many conflicts. It's what will eventually help you step into the color Cobalt (the fifth level), which has to do with building trust, loyalty, respect, and strong team connections.

Building a team by communicating and demonstrating your chosen values can change the game! As we begin this team-building phase, look at the list of words below that capture the *values* Kevin and I promote in our company culture.

- Fairness

- Integrity

- Kindness

- Excellence

- Teamwork

- Health

These apply to everyone involved in the business: team members, patients, vendors, and outside resource people, including our I.T. support and the people who clean the office. In so many workplaces—including ours—these principles are tested. In our case, we hadn't established or communicated the values we wanted at the core of our workplace culture. The communication was just not there. Now that we have developed our clarity and conversations about values, I challenge you to find a more functional, happier, and delightful workplace than Grossmont Vision Center Optometry.

Beginning with the values listed above, let's discuss how to incorporate these into the fabric of your business.

Fairness Is Essential

Oh, the mistakes Kevin and I made in this area!

It seemed like we had risen to this Azure level for a moment, with each person on our team knowing her job description well. Then, Kevin hired a family friend as his assistant, and the team fell apart again in an ugly way.

Jealousy showed up in the office. Since Marisol, Kevin's newly hired assistant, had known Kevin and my family for several years, Kevin's relationship with her was personal and now professional. But, boy, did we learn a lesson about that!

Kevin would carpool in with Marisol every day, and just the optics got the other staff members out of sorts. Also, Marisol's desk was in Kevin's office to help them work closely together. Surprisingly, the opticians who had been sharing an office for years got their hackles up over this apparent "favorite" employee.

Drama (*unending* drama, it seemed) ensued until Marisol finally quit over the poor treatment she received from the other team members. It was painful, but it was for the best. The entire office took a sigh of relief. Time to regroup. Again.

Reflecting on this, we learned that all employees must have a level playing field regarding access to and treatment by the business owner. I believe we have a moral responsibility to treat all our employees fairly. Fairness in the workplace is also critical to your company's success.

Employees who see themselves or their co-workers treated unfairly often experience low employee morale. Everyone witnesses the unfair treatment, even if the offense seems directed at co-workers. Low morale decreases employee productivity every single time.

Fairness in the workplace means treating your employees and everyone with respect and dignity. In other words, treat others the way you want to be treated—the Golden Rule. By reinforcing this principle with your comments and actions, you will create an environment where the employees treat each other fairly and positively.

It is your job to be the diplomat and carefully analyze every employee's salary, benefits, physical setting, and work schedule. The biggest complaint I hear from staff members is that someone with less experience or competency is getting paid disproportionately higher than others in the office. If there were ever a way to make an employee upset and mad, this is it.

As you hire people over time, salaries might lose their logic because you must use current market pay scales. The new employee may enter the company at a higher pay rate than established employees because of market demand. But this cannot stand! There are times when you must pay a higher salary to get a new employee. For fairness, you must also bring the established employees' salaries into line as soon as possible. This policy is how you would want your employer to treat you, right?

The same goes for benefits, physical settings, and work schedules. Nothing will cause more negativity and upset than a staff member who feels his or her boss is being unfair. I don't know if you would learn this by getting an M.B.A. degree, but you realize it quickly in an arbitrary, unjust environment.

Salary and Benefits Need to Make Sense

Money is a sensitive subject for many people. So, should you have complete transparency regarding salaries among your staff? There are pros and cons to doing so. For example, suppose you make the salary information available to everyone. In that case, you must also make the compensation practices you use to *determine* salaries very clear.

On the other hand, what if the employees don't have the "algorithm" you have devised to determine their pay scales? Then the salary discrepancies may not look fair. But if they have all the information (which is a lot to disperse: pay, benefits, job description, industry experience, length of time with the company, performance, etc.), it can bring a team more peace of mind about the fairness of the pay structure.

I don't think you ever need to announce the various team members' salaries and benefits. The most important thing is to let them know your formula for determining their pay and that you care a lot about its fairness. I have worked in enough offices to know that people will always talk among themselves and figure out what others are making. If you pay unequal salaries, word will get around fast. It's not uncommon for employees to share salaries and news about benefits. When they do, there must be a sense of fairness in how salaries and benefits are decided. When every employee sees that he or she will be recognized and rewarded, you cultivate trust, and fairness in the workplace becomes the norm. Although management styles may vary, treating employees with fairness should remain constant.

Of course, fairness matters in all areas, not just salary and benefits. For example, if you always say "yes" to Mary's day-off request but rarely grant Linda's request, you may have *reasons* to do this, but look at it from Linda's point of view. Your team members pay close attention to how you treat their peers, customers, and vendors. Your staff will interpret even the little things, like your mood, facial expressions, tone of voice, and body language. They will use these as clues to how you feel about them and everything going on. Here is where it becomes critical to treat each person in the group with equal respect—more on this at the Amethyst level.

Workplace fairness also includes understanding your employees. You will want to get to know each of them. While you don't want to pry into their personal lives, getting some insight into their challenges and delights will help you see the whole person. For example, if you know one of your employees is going through a hard time at home, you'll likely be able to understand if his or her performance at work suffers. Understanding something about your employees' lives will help keep your relationships with them on good terms. Finally, focus on creating a family atmosphere, which research shows is where everyone, even employers, can thrive.

Ensure fair and logical promotions

Now that we have discussed fairness in employee treatment and salaries, let's talk about promotions. How do you best communicate performance appraisals or promotions without being unfair? How do you choose who to promote? Sometimes, the decision related to promotions shouldn't be up to you (in a sense). People can show you their potential on their own, and all you must do is *notice* it. Following these guidelines has helped us make fair and logical decisions.

Pay attention to employees' personal growth

Even if two of your employees seem to have similar performance reviews, the question is, who's ready for more? When making promotions, consider each of your team players individually before deciding whom to choose for an advancement.

Focus on honing the skills and *then* make your final decision. For example, one of your staff members may be ready for something more challenging (perhaps you will raise her to a management role). At the same time, another may need to learn more from her current position.

Don't judge by past experiences

When you hire someone new, assign a role that might already be comfortable. However, once you build up to an Azure level, try to keep people's resumes out of your mind and focus instead on their performance. Sometimes, the result of giving someone a chance based on their *potential* rather than their experience can surprise you.

Create opportunities for senior positions

Occasionally, all an individual needs is a little push from you to completely transform into a new, more brilliant version of himself. You will want to provide your staff with excellent online courses for them to take, great books for them to read, and exciting seminars for them to attend. These will be highly specific courses that they can put into action. As you spend time with your employee reviewing and implementing his new knowledge, you will bring about a version of that employee who will be even more dedicated to you because you're the one who brought about his transformation! Offer your teammates these valuable resources regularly and see if they grow and expand. If they don't rise to the occasion, what do you lose? But if they do level up, you'll have plenty to gain!

Encourage people from different departments to collaborate

Let people dabble in various jobs. It allows them to develop new skills and helps them become better at their current roles.

An employee at Kimpton Hotels and Restaurants explains:

"Kimpton gives all its employees equal opportunities to enhance their education and cross-train to progress towards their career goals. As vacancies occur, Kimpton

gives internal applicants the first chance. We interview every internal applicant before we consider an external candidate."

This policy adds to the fairness factor.

Cultivate Kindness

Once you have established a genuinely fair environment, you are ready to add to your company's culture. A culture of kindness brings many benefits to a team, as proven by research. In a study by Gallup, higher rates of kindness predicted productivity, efficiency, and lower turnover rates. When leaders and employees act kindly toward each other, they facilitate a culture of collaboration and innovation.

How can leaders promote kindness in the workplace?

The first way is to give sincere compliments. If you hand out praise regularly, you are role-modeling the principle of kindness. In addition, when you praise your employees, your team members will copy your behavior and give sincere kudos and flattering remarks to everyone on the team.

Being recognized at work by one's boss and co-workers

helps an employee experience less burnout and absenteeism and improves employee well-being. Gallup Research finds this result year after year in its surveys of U.S. workers. People are naturally sensitive to the behaviors of their employers and teammates. Receiving a compliment, words of recognition, and praise can help individuals feel more fulfilled. These can boost their self-esteem, improve their self-evaluations, and trigger positive emotions.

Another dimension to kindness is to often speak positive affirmations to your team members that are supportive and encouraging. Phrases like, "Way to go!" or "I understand this is a challenge, but I know you can do it" can be the inspiration your employee might need at that moment. It will also be rewarding for you to hear team members use these affirmations with each other.

Remember to listen actively and improve your communication (covered in detail when we reach the Turquoise level).

Promote excellence

When you follow this guide to creating an Indigo team, excellence will be a natural outcome. All the different levels, and the steps to achieve those levels, will lead you to have an excellent team. Along the way, remember these principles.

Let your mission statement be your guide

Our research has clearly shown two significant problems in organizations with low scores in the "excellence" area. First, they do not have a written, *displayed* mission statement. A person can't be excellent at something when he or she is not even sure what the purpose of the job is. Truly great organizations lead with a compelling, positive vision.

Include your team in making decisions

Top leaders seek out the thoughts and opinions of employees, especially before making changes that impact their work. These leaders expect employees to think about and contribute to decisions that improve the company. This way, the employees feel heard and part of the decision-making process. This inclusiveness stimulates an attitude of excellence because the staff wants to ensure that any team projects they emotionally invest in will succeed. More on this when we cover the Turquoise level and greatness through communication.

Select the right person for the right job

When you interview candidates, getting their views on the *value of excellence* is a good idea. Once you hire them and introduce them to the importance of excellence (and the other Azure team values), you will notice if they are a fit. Look for "green flags" like their ability to communicate quickly and clearly, and the depth of knowledge they display. If they are the right fit for your team, you will also be able to sense their enthusiasm and authenticity.

Nothing is a more unmistakable sign that a person is not suitable for your team than someone who can't live up to the value of excellence or the other company values. If all you can find are mediocre or poor candidates, be patient and keep trying. It is better to wait and repost the job than hire the wrong person.

Create a united team atmosphere

An excellent team is the only thing that will ever produce company success. To consistently win, you need both great players and great teamwork. Each team member must accept responsibility, be accountable, and produce extraordinary results so the team can achieve set goals. There will be more on creating a tightly bonded team in the upcoming section on the Cobalt level.

Expect accountability. The best organizations excel in

performance management by clearly defining what they expect of their employees, giving employees ongoing feedback regarding their performance, and holding all team members accountable for meeting performance standards. Employees need to see the target they are trying to hit.

Insist on Integrity

Kevin and I learned early on from the book *The Millionaire Next Door* that integrity in our business would always be our biggest asset. We emphasized the principle of integrity on Day One with our patients, vendors, and staff. Our mistake was that we never told our team members that we expected them to have 100% integrity in *their* jobs. Now we understand that we must weave the value of integrity through the entire business. This strong message gives the company foundational strength. Without this value, things can get weird.

You would think that opticians, who are such friendly people, who help you choose your eyewear, would not have a problem with integrity. But some of them have been quite dishonest!

With a small group, the tendency can be to get territorial. Also, without good leadership, employees can develop some feelings of competition. It can lead to back-stabbing, bullying, manipulation, sabotage, isolation, hurt feelings, and crying. It sounds more like 8th-grade politics, but this is how a small unmanaged team can disintegrate. The team needs leadership most when it devolves away from integrity.

For example, Lena was an optician with a solid reputation and strong skills. She seemed like a hire we were lucky to have. But a couple of years into her employment, one of the other opticians let us know that Lena was stealing from us! She signed up for deals with vendors that the company paid for and then took the free "extras" home and used them for her benefit. As a result, free San Diego Padres tickets or Bay Cruise tickets would go straight to her without anyone else knowing. So much for the culture of integrity! But we had not yet worked on the company culture at this point.

It was sad to let an employee go, especially one whom we had become fond of, and on whom we relied. Still, we had to stick with our principles and core values and create a culture that reflected our commitment to integrity, no matter how difficult it seemed. We fired Lena, hired a new optician, and began again at the Powder Blue level. This time we emphasized integrity immediately as one of our highest values.

Encourage Teamwork

Once we finalized and announced our newly established values to the staff, our five employees formed a group text where they could check in with each other in the morning. They would offer support to anyone who might be running late or need a last-minute latte. They even named themselves "Working Warriors."

Seeing the team members embrace our principles, such as teamwork and kindness, without me directing these communications was a satisfying (and surprising) business moment. If you speak and exemplify your values to your staff, they will absorb them and start demonstrating them.

Promote teamwork by being involved in your team's work. This active presence will encourage everyone to speak up and take action when a staff member needs help. Since you will illustrate collaborative work, it will become part of the company culture. You will develop a powerful team because "2 + 2 = 5" happens when you get this synergy ball rolling.

Emphasize Good Health

Cultivating a workplace environment centered around healthy habits and good choices is easier than you may think. You don't have to build a gym in your office. However, suppose you offer to pay for a local gym membership for employees. In that case, it might be greatly appreciated and a wise investment.

Research indicates that promoting healthy living can save money in the long run. Studies by Buck Consultants found that saving money is a primary motivation for 74% of companies with wellness programs in place. Secondary benefits include improving productivity, reducing sick days, and retaining workers.

Regularly communicating the value of good health to your staff is the first step in creating an environment that focuses on well-being. Then the more challenging part: role model a healthy lifestyle. For example, if they see you eating fresh fruit and salads, drinking plenty of water, and taking 10-minute mental health breaks, that conveys the message that it is o.k. for them to do the same.

I like to keep a fruit bowl refreshed in the staff break room and provide an abundant source of filtered water. I added a Soda Stream appliance that turns your flatwater into bubbly water. Often, we discuss easy, healthy recipes and restaurants and cafés that offer delicious, fresh food. Also, whenever I can, I like to turn the conversation to the employees' favorite forms of exercise and encourage them to stay active.

Successful companies know that healthy employees are happy employees, and happy employees produce the best work.

These six values are precisely suitable for building the culture that we want. So now, I design culture-building exercises around these values for every staff meeting. Communicating and modeling these principles work so well—you will be amazed.

So, choose wisely and thoughtfully. Then, after contemplating the exact culture you want and visualizing what your day in the office might look like, choose your values and promote them with everything you've got!

❧Fairness Is a Must on an Indigo Team❧

My friend Tony owns an auto repair shop with his father. They employ two mechanics, both of whom are not only excellent at their profession but also great guys. Joaquin had been their shop's first employee; he was hired at a fair rate for the current time, seemed to love his job, and the customers sang his praises. When it came time to hire a second mechanic, the market had changed, and the going hourly rate was several dollars higher per hour than when Tony and his father hired Joaquin. As a result, the new employee made more than Joaquin, who had been there for five years.

Joaquin didn't say anything about the pay discrepancy for a while. Eventually, though, Tony noticed that Joaquin seemed unhappy and was not working with as much enthusiasm as he had before the new mechanic, Mark, had come on board.

Tony felt his budget was already stretched to its limit. But when he consulted me about this situation, I suggested that if he didn't raise Joaquin's salary to meet or exceed Mark's salary, he was handicapping his company's success. No employee can be expected to give 100% if he feels mistreated or under-appreciated. An intelligent business strategy involves making everything equitable and letting the business thrive from that solid foundation. Tony raised Joaquin's pay rate to exceed Mark's pay rate. From then on, Joaquin seemed to give his best.

It's all about the principle of "playing the same game" and

being part of the same team. It has to be fair, or a highly successful Indigo team is impossible.

Key Takeaways

Here's what we can take away from Azure team principles.

- First, choose values you would like your business and team to embrace.

- Consider the core values I suggest, as some are critical for an outstanding team.

- Regularly emphasize the values you have chosen in staff meetings and other communications.

- Put those values into action with your attitudes, words, and behaviors.

Part IV. The Turquoise Team: Communication

"The art of communication is the language of leadership."

↪James C. Humes↩

You have your hand-selected team. Every staff member is trained according to his or her job description and is on board with the values that create your company culture. You are now ready to establish communication methods that will strengthen your team and company. As you enter the Turquoise level, the idea is to build effective lines of communication. Then, you will test them to find the magic communication formula to which your staff responds enthusiastically.

Kevin and I could have avoided several dramatic episodes if only we had developed open channels for team members to tell us their ideas and articulate what they needed from us. Read on for the steps you can take to build an open and honest communication system.

Chapter 9. Communication Is Always the Solution

Open, transparent, two-way communication is fundamental to developing a healthy, harmonious, efficient team.
To begin with, you must have more than one line of communication. Here are essential categories for establishing active communication lines in your business.

- Surveys (Survey Monkey)

- Email

- Text

- Live streaming (Zoom, Skype, etc.)

- In-person F.U.N. monthly staff meetings

- Active listening

- One-on-one monthly performance meetings

- Social media platforms like Slack, Google Chat, Circle

- Hand-written notes

I would include carrier pigeons if I thought it would improve our communication!

Ask for feedback on how individuals and groups (for example, in our case, the people responsible for greeting our customers at the door, which may include team members with various roles) feel about different types of communication. The happier everyone is with the lines of communication, the smoother your team will run. And the more well-connected everyone is, the better your business results will be.

Communication Matters

There's a reason one of the core ingredients of a great personal or intimate relationship is communication. And in business, one of your most important relationships is your relationship with your personnel—the people who will carry your organization forward and are responsible for the outcomes you strive to achieve. So, it's not only crucial that you have clear lines of communication with them, but it's also essential that they communicate well with each other. Effective communication has the power to optimize efficiency, minimize problems, and create an atmosphere of synergy and innovation. It can help increase trust and respect regardless of individual roles and responsibilities. It allows all team members to share their views and ideas and to ask for help when needed.

Building clear lines of communication is one of the most important ways to speed up the trust-building process among your team and boost your company's output. It will also lead to an automatic rise in morale because you can only run a successful business when everyone is on the same page! Let all staff members know that you appreciate when they consistently communicate with you and their co-workers.

Communication is the bread and butter of any great organization. When Kevin and I were trying to put our team back together, it took us a little time to realize the magical healing powers of communication. Did you know scientists tell us that 90% of our communication is body language, including facial expressions? We instinctively know this is true. Do you ever see someone roll his eyes at your idea? Or slump with his head down when discussing his new schedule? Reading body language, and using your body language to express yourself, is a must when working closely with others.

You may think communication would come easy for small

companies, but that isn't always the case. In my experience, people who must work closely together often harbor resentment and hide conflicts, especially when they are not communicating clearly.

Here are some reasons to invest time and effort into making your company's communication top-notch.

Give everyone a voice

Sometimes, all a person needs is to have someone listen. Well-developed lines of communication can go a long way in letting everyone have an outlet for their thoughts or input. It's how we build strong teams.

Foster innovation

If your team can openly communicate ideas without fear of ridicule or retribution, they will be more likely to present new ideas and visions. Innovation and creativity rely on active communication. Our monthly staff meetings have supportive brainstorming sessions where all opinions are allowed and encouraged.

Encourage growth

Talking about new ideas, allowing space for healthy

dissent, and creating a synergistic environment will lead to valuable growth. By communicating with each other, we can grow as individuals and as a team. We learn how to coordinate better when we understand the needs of others.

Develop strong management

As a manager, you'll be much more efficient in delegation, motivation, conflict management, and relationship building if you communicate effectively. These are your critical responsibilities and become much easier once you are a skillful communicator.

❧Extraordinary Communication❧

Jack, a brilliant IT professional, learned that technical expertise only goes so far. After many years of hard work, he rose in his field and eventually earned the role of senior network design engineer for a prestigious technology company. He led multiple small teams across the United States.

Running a huge project opened Jack's eyes to the importance of consistent, clear communication with his teams. His manager had given him the mission of replacing a 10-year-old hospital network system with a new design.

The technical side of this assignment was challenging on its own, but the hardest part was dealing with a dramatic change mid-project.

Jack had launched the project by investing hours and hours into meetings with his staff, his hospital contacts, and their team on the best way to replace a network that spanned six floors and involved 700 network connections.

Everything went well until the hospital client changed the work order in the middle of the project. Jack strongly advised against this change, but his manager sided with the client. It must have felt like being stranded in the middle of a storm.

But Jack didn't give up. He started from scratch, again putting many hours into communicating with everyone on the project. He was constantly on his phone or in Zoom meetings, trying to get his team and the hospital's team on the same page regarding this new track. Some sessions would last several hours, but he hung in there, communicating and coordinating. He admits to using some strong language, but at least he kept communicating.

Jack overcame obstacle after obstacle to complete this project successfully. He listened intently to everyone and never blamed anyone. It was important to him that people on his project knew he had their back.

Jack's extraordinary IT skills were critical in this achievement. Still, he believes his dedication to *communication* made it possible for the hospital to have modern high-speed internet that benefited the patients and medical staff.

Jack's many hours of active listening earned him the respect of everyone involved. He also paid attention to team dynamics, read people's body language, and stayed consistent with daily meetings. I know Jack, so I'm sure his charges and his client's team felt supported, appreciated, and respected.

Chapter 10. Communication Done Right

Everyone Loves a Survey

Surveys allow your employees a chance to express themselves and have their opinions heard—perhaps anonymously. An anonymous survey might bring forth more honesty. Use the survey data to help you understand internal issues your team may face and to guide your actions.

Surveys demonstrate to your team that their feedback and opinions matter to you. The mere act of conducting an employee satisfaction survey can increase employee engagement. One excellent use of employee surveys is to gain insight into your employees' genuine opinions toward your company's benefits program. Doing this is essential because you'll learn what benefits your team appreciates the most and what they want to add. You can then restructure your employee compensation programs based on this factual data.

An employee survey is a diagnostic tool for revealing the strengths and weaknesses of the company. The employees' knowledge of the daily work process can provide helpful information about day-to-day operations. You can then use this data to improve your systems.

Wouldn't you like it if your boss wanted your opinion on various work subjects? Employees feel so validated when you ask them what they think. I send out two surveys each month on various topics, and then we discuss the results at the monthly staff meeting. Everyone is so interested in the survey results! From there, we can make better decisions together. We even decide what kind of Christmas party the staff prefers based on survey results! Surveys can help you retain existing employees and turn them into long-time, loyal team members.

Active Listening Makes All the Difference

Here is my favorite definition of active listening:

Active listening refers to a pattern of listening that keeps you engaged with your conversation partner positively. It is the process of listening attentively while someone else speaks, paraphrasing and reflecting on what is said, and withholding judgment and advice (from the Very Well Mind podcast).

Nothing in the communication category beats active listening! As an entrepreneur, finding the time to really listen to the ideas of everyone around you can be challenging. But ignoring them can be worse. Active listening helps you understand your employees and your business. It also builds trust. You create a strong bond when you become a sounding board and purposefully paraphrase what an individual is communicating. And doesn't everyone love the feeling of being heard?

It might sound easy, but active listening takes a lot of focus, practice, and commitment. When you get good at it, the magic happens! You understand everyone better; they appreciate your presence more because they feel valued.

Here are the basic techniques of being an active listener:

- Repeat back to the speaker what you think she is saying. Say, "What I think I hear you saying is…"

- Allowing the person speaking to have gaps in her words, phrases, and sentences. Be careful to refrain from interjecting before she is done. Be patient, and let silence be okay.

- Demonstrate—with your body language and facial expressions— that you are listening. Maintain eye contact, smile when appropriate, lean toward the person speaking, and mirror his or her body language.

- Be sure not to interject your own experience, advice, or opinion. Stay neutral, and do not judge. Of course, you have ideas about the subject, but this is not the time to express yourself.

- Carefully watch the speaker's body language and facial expressions, and listen to his or her tone of voice to pick up more information.

- When you reply to a person, stay on the subject. Respond with empathy and understanding.

- Ask questions about that subject. Don't focus on the little things; keep the big picture in mind. What is the other person saying? What is he or she feeling?

- When the person has finished communicating with you, summarize what you think he or she is trying to say. If the person corrects you, take in the correction and summarize again.

Active listening is the exact opposite of passive hearing.

Here are some things that passing hearing involves (these are the DON'Ts):

- You are looking at your phone, computer, watch, out the window, etc. Passive hearers become distracted. Instead, maintain eye contact with the person sharing.

- You are interrupting the person speaking. Passive hearers do this ALL the time.

- Jumping in with "that reminds me of…" Don't tell your own stories; stay focused on what the person is saying. (This is the most difficult one for me).

- You are thinking of what you will say next in response instead of focusing only on what the person is saying. Shut down your internal dialogue!

It might take a while to master this technique (I'm still working on it), but the rewards will be great.

Make Staff Meetings Fun

Research shows that communication and team-building interventions such as staff meetings are effective and positively affect the perceptions and attitudes of team members (Tannenbaum et al. 1992).

I wanted our staff to look forward to our monthly meetings instead of dreading them (which most teams do), so Kevin and I now purchase lunch as part of the meeting. I also bring in some gourmet bakery items and some scratch-off lottery tickets. During the gathering, we give the staff plenty of space to express their feelings about their roles.

I'm always open to discovering new techniques to jazz up a meeting! The strategies below work and our staff members now look forward to and love staff meetings.

Holding regular team meetings is an excellent way to connect with your employees. These gatherings should be a safe space for your team to share new ideas, brainstorm, and collaborate on projects. However, meetings about reports, numbers, and financial goals can get dull quickly!

So, the question is, exactly how do you make your team look forward to staff meetings?

Make them fun! There are many creative ways to add more energy to regular meetings and make them more productive.

Here are some ways you can make meetings fun:

Keep the ball rolling

Keep your team engaged and empowered by constantly encouraging their feedback on matters and actively involving them in decision-making. So, in meetings, keep the ball rolling. Ask questions and update your team on the subjects that matter to them.

High energy is contagious

We will discuss high energy in our seventh and final stage, Indigo. But for now, you need to know how influential high vibrations can be. Suppose all you do as their leader is bring energy and positivity to your meetings. In that case, you will be setting the tone for everyone else. You are also likely to transfer that energy to the people around you. Lead by example with the spirit you bring!

Add ice breakers

You can make meetings fun by playing games and asking

fun questions to keep your team on their toes and engaged with each other. Start the session by breaking the ice with some getting-to-know-each-other questions and games. These activities help everyone learn more about each other and lead to fun conversations, laughter, and bonding.

Ice-breaker activities are personal and fun. We ask for the staff's thoughts and feelings. But ice-breaker questions are about getting to know someone better.

Sample questions

- What is your favorite snack food and beverage? Do you prefer coffee or tea? Would you choose popcorn or chips while watching a movie? Do you like sweet or salty flavors?

- What's your favorite part of your job—and why?

- What's your favorite hobby?

- What is one dare-devil activity you have always wanted to try?

- What is the favorite birthday present you've ever received?

- Ask everyone to share one TV series or movie recommendation. Most of us are always on the hunt for the next binge-worthy series.

For extra fun, turn on some music and get the whole team moving for a dance party (this is also effective for online meetings).

Show and tell

Show and tell isn't just for children; adults enjoy it, too. It encourages people to showcase their personalities and parts of their lives that are important to them! Whether your colleagues want to talk about their work, homes, families, pets, or hobbies, it's an excellent opportunity for individuals to work on their presentation skills creatively. Consider assigning one person per meeting for show and tell. This exercise provides a perfect opportunity to get to know one another better, fostering stronger interpersonal relationships with a means to connect over subjects that aren't work-related. Often, we don't even know what people do outside of the office! Getting to know one another more personally will foster more genuine relationships.

Celebrate wins

Staff meetings are a great time to celebrate team wins. Highlight your team's accomplishments and show your employees that their contributions are valuable to the organization. You will motivate your team to continue performing at a high level by giving public praise and encouraging them to hit goals and milestones. Get specific about the team wins, reviewing and emphasizing precisely what took place. Read any positive customer feedback and reviews out loud and give credit where credit is due. Then talk about the current milestones you are working toward collectively.

Include shoutouts

Dedicate a section of the meeting agenda for people to add shoutouts for their colleagues (i.e., thanking people for their help). Shoutouts are a great way to lift team spirits and encourage collaboration, making team members feel seen, heard, and appreciated. It is essential because individuals may need to realize the weight of their impact and efforts. In addition, this practice will encourage team members to continue to go above and beyond for their colleagues, promoting better communications, more collaboration, and fostering better workplace relationships.

Play games

Playing fun games is a great way to engage everyone and focus on something lighter than the usual organizational discussions. Trivia games such as Kahoot and Trivial Pursuit are great options to engage the team and get individuals to work together to have fun. The game Jenga also gets lively as each person removes a wooden piece from a tower while trying not to let it collapse.

Many games encourage us to use valuable skills, such as critical thinking abilities, creativity, strategizing, and attention to detail. It is an excellent opportunity for team members to use different and unique skills to come together in a lightly competitive environment.

Bring gifts and goodies

This technique gets positive feedback! If one staff member is a good baker and enjoys baking, give him or her some petty cash to fund the treats. Or stop by the bakery.

Also, giving the same small gift to everyone can add a lot to the enjoyment factor. These offerings are tokens of appreciation. Use your imagination and creativity to pick out what they all might find pleasing. For example, I bought lottery tickets one month, and we all scratched them off together. Another month I bought small organic soy candles for each person. It makes the meeting feel like a special occasion.

How to Review Individual Job Performance

Staff meetings are solely for team communications. The group can discuss triumphs and trials together in a relaxed atmosphere. The team can consider company goals and problem-solving, even while having fun. But at regular intervals, you must also address each individual's performance. This gets more serious because a team is only as strong as its weakest link.

Communication never becomes more important in a business than reviewing your employee's performance. The old-fashioned way of conducting annual one-on-one job performance meetings is no longer viable. This was the common practice at Standard Oil/Chevron and American Airlines when I worked there. It was always, frankly, ridiculous! Once a year is not nearly often enough to be clear about how things are going and how to make course corrections if needed. Fortunately, today's job performance meetings are a more organic, spontaneous process. They are no longer the dreaded "annual review" known for being a one-way conversation.

The best way to review an employee's performance is to meet face-to-face once a month. That way, a course correction, if needed, can happen soon. But what if you want to make an immediate change? Meeting with any of your staff privately at a moment's notice is always an option available to you. Be polite and respectful and ask, "Will you do this for me?" or "I have a favor to ask." Then, after explaining the correction, say something like, "Do you agree?" Then use active listening. Remember that you always deal with job performance issues in private settings. Give praise, support, and encouragement when others can hear.

Sometimes you will want to correct or re-train the entire staff on something that applies to everybody, like how to greet people on the phone or when they walk in the door. Then, you can incorporate that training into a staff meeting or call a standing daily huddle. A standing daily huddle is where the team stands in a circle and goes over the day's upcoming challenges and goals. You direct the conversation and listen but keep the meeting between five and ten minutes. Suppose they go longer, or one person constantly dominates the conversation. In that case, the team members will start to dread the standing huddle. Yet this method is valuable for setting the day's intentions, making group course corrections, and preparing for what the day brings.

Sometimes, you'll pull aside a group of co-workers who share specific roles (in our case, it may be the opticians) to go over something you want them to do a little better or a little differently.

None of these methods of speaking to someone about job performance includes any harshness, as if you're that old cliché of a jerk kind of a boss. You know, the guy who criticizes people and makes them feel bad, maybe to boost his own ego? That's not you, and it's definitely not what your team needs. Those on your team are like royalty to you. Even when they make mistakes (even costly ones), you respectfully fix the problem. You know that everything is ultimately your responsibility.

ঌCommunication in Action: Victor's Storyৎ

Victor, a likable young man whose family had migrated from Vietnam, is in charge of event planning at a beautiful private university. He has a knack for treating everyone respectfully, which has helped in his career.

In his role at the university, Victor began each project by finding out precisely what the client wanted and then relaying that specific information to his team, which could vary in size from five to thirty people, depending on the event.

When Victor began his job, he experienced some events turning into big, chaotic messes. At times, he felt like pulling his hair out and crying! But he quickly learned that the cause of these disasters was poor communication. He began putting more effort into communicating with his teams; he came up with an intelligent communication system I have since adopted. Victor describes it in three steps:

1. The Active Feedback Loop

When Victor tells a teammate what it is he wants him or her to accomplish, he states, in his own words, precisely the vision the client has expressed. Then, he asks that teammate to describe the vision, but in the teammate's own words. Victor doesn't want the employee to parrot back what he or she heard; Victor wants to listen to the message restated by the employee. He says this clears up a multitude of misunderstandings.

2. The Visual

After communicating the client's vision in an active feedback loop, Victor ensures he provides his team with visuals. Whether it's a drawing, a photograph, a social media post, or a video, Victor believes in the saying, "A picture is worth a thousand words." As a result, the client's vision is now further clarified for the team.

3. Concise Instructions

The final step in achieving a client's vision is writing a quick list of instructions. He keeps it concise, no longer than the size of a post-it note or 3 x 5 card. Because the instructions are clearly articulated, Victor has confidence the event will go splendidly.

These communication tools make Victor's events run smoothly and reflect each client's vision. Nonetheless, he still emphasizes to his team that there can never be enough communication between him and all the other team players. I call Victor a Turquoise level Master Manager.

Key Takeaways

- Effective communication is an absolute must in creating a successful team.

- Figure out, maintain, and manage active lines of communication.

- Use surveys so your team members have a voice in company decisions.

- Practice active listening.

- Conduct fun and productive staff meetings.

- Conduct job performance reviews regularly and in the right way.

Part V. The Cornflower Team: Physical Environment

"The physical workspace is where we breathe and live every day of our work lives. It affects everyone who enters. When the quality of life is at stake, you know it's essential."

❧Valerie C. Riggs❦

The physical aspect of your business is so essential that you should attend to it sooner rather than later. As we advance to the Cornflower level, you'll learn why this is vitally important.

Whether you're a founder setting up an office for a startup or a real estate broker building a small firm, you will need a space to operate. Optimizing this space for your team is one of the best strategic moves you can make. In addition, a mostly one-time investment will benefit you in the future because furniture and equipment don't retire quickly.

When Kevin first purchased Grossmont Vision Center, he loved its location (a bustling shopping center) and outdoor access. It seemed like enough space, though he knew it might be tight. The actual physical space and how we used it greatly impacted how our team functioned.

Even though we had some good management practices in place, our team was still mediocre at this point. We had built a foundation, knew our values, and established good communication methods. Then something happened that we didn't expect.

The office suite next door became available, and we had a chance to grab an extra 600 square feet of new office space. We signed the lease and launched a much-needed office remodel. We were excited about our new space.

However, we didn't expect the environment to become chaotic. The construction crew ripped entire walls apart, and then the space was re-carpeted, re-painted, and re-furnished. As items were lost or damaged, and computers and medical equipment that had been relocated were no longer functioning correctly, nerves frayed.

Just as the frustration reached its peak, our most senior optician quit! It seemed a disaster at first, but it turned out to be a blessing. As the office space came back together, we hired a new optician, and guess what? Our remaining optician demonstrated "mean girl" behavior to the new optician, who was knowledgeable and energetic. We witnessed crying, hurt feelings, and general upset between the two opticians until we let the established, "mean girl" optician go. At this point, we had only one of our original four employees left, and the physical space was better but not complete.

We hired one more optician and another new employee (a technician) since we now had more space. Finally, we were ready to start *again* at the Powder Blue level. The remodel was almost complete; all that was left was art for us to hang on the wall. We had a new office and new staff—time for team building again.

And this time, finally, we gained some traction. The new staff was excited about the beautiful new office and happy with the new workstations. Again, Kevin and I addressed comfort, clutter, lighting, noise, air quality, and office temperature until we were sure everything was right.

The remodel shook out some team members and brought a new, more harmonious, motivated, and talented team. The physical space where your team performs its work is Cornflower team territory. The physical environment impacts employee engagement, workplace enthusiasm, productivity, and creativity. I think it can even be a deal-breaker in some cases, as I've seen it happen. Business owners often experience rising absenteeism, turnover, and diminished productivity when they fail to attend to the quality of physical space.

What do you see around you when you come to work each day? Dull walls with paint peeling off and outdated equipment? Stained ceiling tiles and obnoxious fluorescent lighting? Or colorful, modern, clean spaces with beautiful artwork, plants, and flowers, in an overall morale-boosting environment? The difference could determine how dedicated your team is to your business and how each team member feels about working with you.

Yes, it will require some investment, but the return will be worthwhile and the outcome rewarding. Giving people a workspace they *want* to come to every day can be the best way to encourage a team's full potential and capabilities.

I know many people who delay this step for the longest time, thinking it's not as important as their current workload. Eventually, it just never gets done. You will have to actively decide to invest in your physical space if it needs to be changed or updated. It must become part of your budget, to-do list, and schedule.

Even a tiny shift in well-being can dramatically impact the bottom line. There is a reason companies like Google have invested so heavily in their employees' physical space. These companies can see how profitable this type of investment is.

So, the question remains, *how can you create such a physical space for your team, and what aspects should you prioritize?*

Welcome to the Cornflower level, where we talk about all of that. Let's examine how you can create a beautiful, brilliant physical space.

Chapter 11. Spiffing Up the Space

When you create or re-create a space for your Cornflower team, first consult your staff, whose feedback is indispensable throughout this process. Explore the challenges your team faces in your current office. Ask how this space can better serve the team's needs.

Invite employees to participate in focus groups or conduct a survey to understand how people like to work. Do they want to congregate in large, open spaces or prefer a more formal private meeting room? Is a break room useful? Do they prefer to work in cubicles, private offices, or shared workspaces in an open floor plan?

Once you have their input, you can review suggestions to determine the next steps. Remember that you can't possibly expect to implement every recommendation. However, all team members must feel included in the process.

You and your team will spend most of your time in this office space, so it is a mistake not to invest in it. This space should reflect your workplace culture; you will want to design it to make everyone feel welcome and comfortable. Even if you must completely redesign your facilities, trust me when I say this is the secret to productivity and team spirit. An Indigo team cannot happen without its unique workplace.

You will want to continue changing and upgrading your environment over time based on what your employees need and like. And because you are already above the Turquoise level (communication), your team will let you know what modifications should happen next.

Make a Floor Plan

There are quite a few critical decisions that determine your best office layout. First, you will want to decide on dividing public and private areas and how to divide the space for maximum comfort, appeal, and efficiency.

Your floor plan will also depend on your business and how your team members spend most of their time in the office. For example, do they need meeting rooms to collaborate and work in groups? Do they need to move around often or remain stationed at one desk? You may need a mixture of quiet areas and lounge areas.

The layout of an office is an extension of your business' brand. It can say as much about your company as your product or service.

To be effective when designing the layout, carefully consider the flow of day-to-day operations. For example, the floor plan must account for the correct number of workstations, where to position the reception desk, and how big that desk should be. In a retail business, you must figure out customer seating areas, sales, and meeting and training areas. Think carefully about the customer experience you want to create. Also, give your staff plenty of room to do their jobs; no one wants stuffy, cramped quarters. The workspace you provide will significantly impact how your Cornflower team thinks, works, feels, and conducts themselves. By creating spaces that prioritize your team's mental health, there can be improvements in focus, collaboration, and creativity.

For instance, you could add a relaxation space for your employees to de-stress during their breaks. This area could also be a place to socialize or engage in fun activities. By offering people a spot to recharge, companies positively impact employee well-being.

The old way of using cubicles in an office space is entirely *out*! Instead, we want open, cool rooms, opportunities for movement, and areas that organically promote collaboration. Taking down some walls may help with this. Or you could create a circular floor plan that includes the entire team, and everyone is always engaged. Work with all the options until you feel the floor plan is just right.

Let There Be Light

Lighting is more important than anything else when we talk about functional spaces. It affects many aspects of work life, including productivity, mental health, and workplace safety. For example, Harvard Business Review reported that access to natural light and views of the outdoors far outranked other office perks such as fitness centers, cafeterias, or daycare.

I cannot overstate the importance of catching some sunshine during the workday. Many excellent research studies prove this beyond a shadow of a doubt. For example, according to the National Renewable Energy Lab research, natural light significantly increases energy, creativity, and productivity. In addition, workers exposed to natural lighting stayed on task for 15% longer than their sun-deprived counterparts.

Moreover, natural light can dramatically improve mood, boost vitamin D levels, and support the body's circadian rhythms. Cornell University found that office workers with natural daylight reported an 84% decrease in headaches, eye strain, and blurred vision.

According to research by Northwestern University in Chicago, natural light improves sleep: people exposed to direct sunlight gain an average of 46 minutes of sleep at night.

If someone's desk doesn't have a direct window view, encourage him or her to take a walk during the day or sit for a few minutes in the sunshine.

When natural light is not an option, consider using layers of different types of lighting in a workspace, such as task lighting. It will allow you to localize lighting and provide the right amount of light needed to suit various tasks.

There are so many options in modern commercial lighting! From LED lighting to commercial fluorescents to halogen lighting. According to the experts, the best lighting for success and productivity is cool lighting, similar to the color of the midday sun.

This cool lighting is a cornerstone for office productivity because it supports mental acuity and vitality. This type of lighting inhibits melatonin production, a hormone that makes you feel sleepy, thus decreasing fatigue and daytime tiredness. Evidence suggests that spending time under blue-enriched light during your workday is as effective as utilizing bright light treatment for seasonal affective disorder (SAD).

Be sure to prioritize the entire lighting system in your office space. From window coverings to overhead lights to lamps on desks and other task lighting, be aware of how you can improve lighting for everyone's benefit.

Spare No Expense for Comfort and Productivity

An ergonomic workplace design can reduce physical problems such as carpal tunnel syndrome, backaches, and neck pain. The definition of ergonomics is "designed to minimize physical effort and discomfort and hence maximize efficiency."

Below are some ergonomic best practices from the Mayo Clinic. Encourage everyone in your office to follow these instructions:

- Make sure to center your body in front of your monitor and keyboard. Sit up straight, keeping your thighs horizontal with your knees at about the same level as your hips. Keep your forearms level or tilted up slightly.

- Adjust the height of the office chair so that your feet rest comfortably on the floor. If the chair doesn't offer lumbar support, place a cushion between the curve of your lower back and the back of the chair.

- If you frequently talk on the phone and type or take notes simultaneously, use a headset rather than cradling the phone between your head and neck. Experiment with various styles until you find the headset that works best for you.

- Use a wrist rest to minimize stress on your wrists and prevent awkward wrist positions. While using a keyboard, place your hands and wrists on the wrist rest. During breaks, rest the heels or palms of your hands—not your wrists—on the wrist rest.

- Place your monitor directly in front of you, about an arm's length—generally 18 to 28 inches—away. The top of the screen should be slightly below your eye level.

Ergonomic desks, chairs, and accessories support posture and comfort the users. Choosing comfortable ergonomic furnishings and related items is worth your time and money.

Make the Space Beautiful

When planning an office layout and design, the decorating style and overall appearance are important factors.

Being in a comfortable, inviting atmosphere dramatically impacts our overall mood and productivity. But did you know that a beautiful interior design for your office space can also impact the success of your business? Likewise, learning how to decorate an office properly can significantly affect your business.

The most productive offices balance the comforts of home with a professional business image. You'll want it to be a stylish setting full of color, life, and inspiration, leading to a happy, healthy work environment for your team members to thrive.

Your office design ideas should embody your company's values to make everyone feel great. You don't want people walking into the office with a wrong first impression because the office design needs a facelift.

Take these decorating ideas below on how to adorn your office with elements that keep you and your team productive, inspired, and motivated every day. It's time to spice up your corporate office design ideas!

- Make your mission statement visible. Think about creating an enlarged image of your company's mission statement and logo and displaying it in a central area.

- Incorporate your brand colors. These colors give you an identifiable look. Your space will present a consistent style that reflects your values.

- Paint an accent wall. To add some look-at-me color to your space without overwhelming your senses, paint one wall with a bright or accent color, and leave the rest of the office lighter and more neutral.

- Add a splash of color (like the accent wall and flowers above). Color can be such a powerful communication tool if you use it correctly. It can directly influence mood and psychological reactions. For example, we associate specific colors with responses like increased blood pressure, metabolism, and eyestrain. However,

VeryWellMind.com reports that natural colors like green evoke optimism and compassion.

- Similarly, orange can be very attention-grabbing, radiating warmth. In contrast, white can convey cleanliness and simplicity. Still, it may also seem stark, cold, and isolated. Therefore, when selecting colors, think about the purpose and function of the space you're creating and then match the color to align with your brand.

- Hang art on the walls. Putting up art can make your workspace look more attractive, thoughtful, and finished. You might want to keep it simple with black and white wall hangings or go bold with vibrant, eye-catching pieces that brighten your day as you walk past them. Adding art to your office walls can be a beautiful expression of creativity to represent your company's heart and mind. The effect will be stunning.

Remember the Little Things

Set the right room temperature

Setting the right temperature for your office promotes the best possible physical workspace.

Have you ever been to an event where the conference room was too cold? Maybe the air conditioner was on a full-blast setting, and you found yourself unable to focus. Or you may remember taking an exam where the exam room was so warm that you lost your train of thought. You might have struggled with the exam because all you could think about was how hot it was in that room.

I hope you won't take it lightly when I say that the right office temperature is essential. It can impact how well we perform or how productive we are. And suppose it's hot or cold enough to distract your employees. In that case, all your other efforts in "decorating" the office space become futile. What's the point of the colorful walls and bean bag chairs when all you want is a blanket or a bucket of ice?

In an article on the "never-ending battle" about office temperature, the BBC reported that "Getting the temperature right can boost job satisfaction, productivity, and collaboration."

Some studies show that warmer temperatures foster creativity, while a colder environment can increase productivity. And interestingly, men and women have different temperature needs. Due to relatively slower metabolic rates and hormones, women feel chilly easier than men. So, what can you do if there is no "right" temperature?

Temperature preferences vary according to individuals. You could always offer items to help each person feel more comfortable in the physical workspace. For instance, you could have portable fans near the desks of those who feel too warm. Or allow the overly warm people to work near windows that let in a cool breeze. For those who feel too cold, provide space heaters or throw blankets.

I try to set the thermostat to the perfect temperature. Then I ask how that setting works for each staff member (either in person or in a survey). Then I adjust up or down according to the team's feedback.

Make clean, fresh air a priority

It's no surprise that air quality in an office is often poor. With so many people working in such a small space, dirt, dust, and other debris can accumulate.

Office renovations or new building construction nearby can affect the air. Poor office air quality can lead to employees with headaches, respiratory problems, coughing, or fevers.

These could be due to an indoor air quality issue, especially if these symptoms occur at work and clear up when people get home.

There's no doubt about the positive impact that fresh air has on our ability to focus and how the opposite can often hinder our workflow. The World Green Building Council highlighted an 11% increase in productivity when employers increased fresh air at workstations.

Luckily, there are ways to improve air quality and keep employees happy and healthy.

Keep your air vents open and unblocked

If furniture, boxes, or other items block the path of your air vents, the air inside your office won't circulate properly and could cause health issues. If there are any signs that your air ducts impact air quality or circulation, get them cleaned by experts. You don't want to wait until someone's health is compromised.

Replace air filters frequently

Over time, dust and debris will build up behind the filters and settle inside the air ducts, putting your employees' health at risk. As a rule, you should replace air filters every six to 12 months.

Maintain a healthy level of humidity

Keep humidity between 30% and 50% for the best and most comfortable environment. You will want to purchase a hygrometer for about $15 on Amazon to test the humidity level. It will show you whether you need to raise or lower the humidity in your office. Suppose your office humidity does not fall in the ideal range. In that case, you may consider a humidifier, which adds extra moisture to the air, or a dehumidifier, which removes excess moisture from the air.

Add a humidifier to the office if your humidity falls below 30%. A dehumidifier will be your solution if your humidity is above 50%. Either way, the people in your office might experience minor allergies and asthma symptoms if the humidity is too high or low. You can expect symptoms like sneezing, coughing, wheezing, a runny nose, and itchy eyes if the humidity is not in the optimal range. If the air moisture is in the desired range, there will be fewer allergy and asthma triggers like mold, dust mites, and pollen.

Other steps to keep your office inviting and healthy include:

- Clean spills immediately. Excess moisture or residual dampness supports the growth of mildew and mold, which can cause severe health risks. Remember that it's more expensive to remediate mold damage than prevent it.

- Add some office plants. They add a pleasing, peaceful aesthetic to any office. They also absorb toxins and produce more oxygen so employees can breathe more easily. All it takes is a few low-maintenance plants to make your space greener.

- Use fresh air whenever possible. If your office has windows that open, let the fresh air flow freely! When weather permits, keeping your windows and doors open helps circulate fresh air in and stale air out.

- Keep your office clean. Regularly vacuum, dust, sanitize, clear away clutter, promptly dispose of all garbage as it accumulates, or hire a janitorial service. It is best to schedule regular professional cleanings to ensure this crucial indoor air quality component isn't overlooked.

- Have your air quality tested. Experts in air quality have the right tools. They know how to measure air quality in offices—from the airflow to humidity levels, ventilation, odors, leaks, standing water, water damage, and mold growth. After a thorough inspection, you will know what to fix to improve office air quality.

❧ The Power of a Beautiful Environment ❧

I have a friend who has a beautiful daughter named Amelia. My friend and her husband were stunned when Amelia decided not to attend college. After some soul-searching, Amelia decided that she wanted to be a yoga instructor; she entered the business world debt-free and brimming with excitement.

Amelia invested two hundred hours into training for a prestigious yoga certification and then threw herself into her business. She had some quick successes, like teaching several weekly classes at a stunning five-star resort. Her engaging style caught the interest of private clients whom she trained in their homes. But in the spring of 2020, she found herself up against a formidable obstacle.

In 2020, the world went digital, and Amelia had no space, equipment, or know-how to record her classes and post them online. Teaching yoga face-to-face with real, live people is all she had done in her career and all she had ever intended to do.

But she knew she had to face reality.

At first, she tried filming herself by propping up her iPhone while she taught her class in a small area of her apartment. Next, Amelia taught herself technical skills with YouTube videos and felt ready to post her classes.

She felt crushed when she got very few "likes" and almost no comments on her classes day after day, month after month. Amelia felt like the digital world had defeated her.

Then she had an idea.

Amelia could see that the backdrop for her yoga classes was not eye-catching enough to compete in a saturated market. After studying other successful yoga instructors on YouTube, Amelia created her own brand. She would film her classes outdoors in natural water environments. Her brand emphasized joy, beauty, fun, and adventure.

Amelia's online classes began to catch on as she improved her filming ability and invested in the proper equipment. Her team grew and loved helping her find the most visually stunning places around San Diego. Amelia's husband helped her film at the San Diego Harbor with gorgeous 50-foot yachts behind her. The last I saw, that video had over 4,000 views! She has gone on to film at many different beaches, bays, and lakes.

Amelia recognizes the power of the physical environment better than any businessperson I know. When the world felt "closed down," she brought the outdoor environment into her videos, creating a brand that offered yoga instruction and a virtual breath of fresh air.

Key Takeaways

- The physical environment is a high priority for a happy, harmonious team.

- Each team member needs his or her space set up with care.

- Each team member requires an individual workstation.

- Integrate your brand's theme into your workspace, if possible, to be more impactful.

- Your physical surroundings should reflect your culture and values.

- Budget for office health and comfort and see the investment pay off in productivity.

- Decorate to inspire creativity and innovation.

Part VI. The Cobalt Team: Team Member Bonding

"Find a group of people who challenge and inspire you, spend a lot of time with them, and it will change your life."

&Amy Poehler&

After finishing a grueling office remodel and a dramatic shift in our staff, we faced the fact that we were starting our team-building project all over again. While Kevin focused on his patients, I was single-minded now that I had confidence in my color-coded plan. I began again at Powder Blue, where we emphasized the mission and clarified the job descriptions. With time and energy, the team moved through each level to the Cornflower level, where our physical environment supported us. It was time to take on the Cobalt level and bond as a team. Team interaction was about to take center stage. Cobalt is all about building strong team connections.

Kevin and I had never done anything like this before, which gave me anxiety! What if it was awkward or boring to get together outside of work? Worse yet, what if it somehow created drama?

But it was time for positive thinking, courage, and determination.

My first step in helping to build the Cobalt realm was to send the staff a survey (to be answered anonymously) to determine what the staff members might like to do as a team activity. I had mentioned this team interaction project at a staff meeting, and the staff gave me some suggestions. The options were: bowling, happy hour cocktails, a bayside picnic, or a visit to a local landmark such as Cabrillo National Park in San Diego.

They chose a picnic! Time to take the team to the Cobalt level, where bonding matters.

I kept it simple. We closed the office early on an agreed-upon date and enjoyed a gorgeous Friday afternoon. I brought everyone's sandwich and beverage orders to the park and set up a picnic table in the shade by the bay.

My nerves were a bit on edge as the start time approached. But as each team member arrived, I felt calmer because seeing the team outside the office was fun. We talked, ate, laughed, and relaxed. At the end of the afternoon, we were a closer team.

The following Monday, I could feel the shift. It was a type

of energy, but if I had to guess, it felt more familiar among the team members. Best of all, that Monday, we had a record-setting day in gross sales. *Coincidence?*

The team grew closer as we continued to participate in bonding activities once a quarter. Everyone seemed to soften and let down his or her walls a bit. The feeling became more like a family vibe. I observed interactions closely at our next event as we laughed at the bowling alley and again during an outdoor seaside concert. The laughter, the sharing of stories and photos, and the fun we had together made me hopeful that this was finally the team that could make it to Indigo.

The success we began having in the office encouraged me that I was on the right track. Kevin was happy with the profit numbers, but one day, I got a phone call from him, and his happiness had disappeared.

"I just can't take it anymore!" I was disappointed to hear him sound this upset again, especially after all the work we had put into building this team with my new system.

"What's the matter?" I asked.

"There are just too many situations to keep up with. The

staff gets their own bright ideas and makes up their own systems, chaos ensues, and I'm in over my head."

That is when I knew what we needed to solve his current problem and take us to the Indigo team level. We needed an office manager. Luckily, I found an excellent optician with practice management experience. She quickly fit right in, and we became a team of five.

Chapter 12. Build an Even Stronger Company Culture

The goal is to build a team whose members trust and respect each other and are loyal to each other and the company.

As the owner or manager, keeping your word is the best way to build trust. When you align your actions with your promises, people notice. They will trust you more each time they witness your consistency. On the other hand, if you don't deliver on what you promised, it causes distrust. If this happens, apologize, make it up to them, and do better next time.

The Golden Rule is to treat others as you want others to treat you. I would also recommend the Platinum Rule: treat others how they would like you to treat them.

You will gain loyalty when you demonstrate to your team that you are on their side. For example, defend your employees if a customer, vendor, or fellow employee unfairly criticizes them. Make it known that you are looking out for them and protecting them.

So how do you build trust, respect, and loyalty in the workplace? Lead by example and encourage these principles.

1. Listen more than you speak.

2. Ask for and act on feedback.

3. Show appreciation for fellow teammates every day.

4. Practice patience and empathy.

5. Be honest and transparent.

Team Events and Activities to Promote Bonding

Nothing speaks louder about an organization's culture than the leader's behavior. If you say teamwork is essential, reinforce that by giving your team time together and time with you. One way to do this is through team-building activities.

Give your team space to relax and interact. Be sure to do this on a schedule, like once a month or once a quarter.

Without segments of time dedicated explicitly to refocusing and reconnecting, things can quickly fall apart, people can get stressed, and a smooth flow can go out the window. Instead, by giving your team space to unwind and regroup periodically, you can allow them to concentrate on the team's priorities and keep everyone's spirits high.

For instance, you could dedicate every Friday to social meetings where you make a point of sitting down together and discussing your weekly wins and losses. Maybe once a month, everyone would enjoy a seasonal activity. In the fall season, head to a pumpkin patch. A more significant event like a music concert or professional ball game might be what bonds your team best. You'll know the right mix of activities and events from the surveys you send them.

What is the foundation for building excellent teamwork? I believe it starts with establishing familiarity, which grows into mutual trust and respect. To help you make your team-building activities effective and enjoyable, here are a few tips that will elevate your efforts.

Plan Regularly Scheduled Activities

Team-building games are a fun and creative way to bring your team together. After trying different scenarios, I always send out a survey to determine what the staff members thought of each activity. The participants are usually clear with their opinions! Over time, you'll find your team's favorites and rule out the less popular games.

When hosting these team-building activities, you must know how to run them. Be clear on the game's objective, what items are required, and how the process works. Nothing puts a group off from these bonding activities more than a botched procedure where the host doesn't know what she is doing or does not have what she needs to execute the game. Be polished as the host and bring your best organizing skills and a fun attitude.

Here are four team-building activities that my staff currently enjoys and on which I receive good feedback:

The "Mad, Sad, Glad" game

Go around the room and ask each participant, "What are you mad about?" then, "What are you sad about?" and "What are you glad about?" This can be set up to include the participant's personal life. The mad, sad, and glad game sometimes brings up unexpected emotions! Pay attention to the answers so that they can be addressed at an appropriate time if they relate to work.

The group timeline

On a surface that accepts thumbtacks, like a cork bulletin board, create a blank timeline. The timeline should start when the most senior employee was born or when the company was founded, whichever came first—mark each year on the timeline. Then, using narrow strips of paper (I cut up colorful post-it notes), write down important dates for the company (like when it was founded, incorporated, introduced a new product, etc.) and pin it to the correct spot on the timeline. Then give your team members four slips of paper and ask each to mark down four important moments in his or her life. Let them pin them to the timeline. This exercise helps show, in a visual way, the different generations and experiences of your team. It leads them to talk about cultural and generational differences and their effects on how people work and communicate. It is also an opportunity for team members to learn more about the company and each other, which creates even more bonding.

"Office Trivia" game

You will need 20-25 trivia questions about your company. Come up with this series of questions specific to your workplace and test your team's knowledge. "What was the name of the previous owner?" "How many employees has the company had in total?" "How many plants are there in the entire office?" "What brand are the computer monitors?" "What month of the year is most common for birthdays among our employees?" Make it a contest, have fun, and give a prize to the winner.

The "Human Knot" game

This game has stood the test of time and is my favorite. All it requires are willing players and open space! The number of players can range from four to 20. Depending on the number of people in your group and the complexity of the human knot you make, this exciting problem-solving game will usually take around 15 to 20 minutes. The team must make good use of their communication abilities, their collaboration abilities, their flexibility (sometimes both mentally and physically), and sense of humor because this game can generate a lot of laughter. It needs to be well run and have a host who gives clear instructions for safety.

You and your team will circle up, standing next to each other. After you're in your circle, reach out and hold hands with two different people in the circle, excluding the two people who are to either side of you. Each left hand should hold a left hand, and each right hand a right. The game's goal is to untangle yourselves from a "human knot" without letting go of the hands you are holding.

Using your best communication skills, figure out how to untangle the knot as a group. Bend, twist, step through, turn around but don't let go of hands. Duck under other players' hands, step over a pair of hands, and figure out the moves to untangle.

As your knot becomes untangled, you'll notice that a circle will again start to form. Some people may end up facing the inside of the circle, some the outside, but by the time you've finished untangling, you should have an unbroken circle of joined hands. Congratulations! You've untangled the Human Knot!

Choose Fun Events for the Entire Team

What if you closed your office one day a month or a quarter for a team-bonding event outside the office on paid time? If this is not practical, you can have your event when the office is closed and the employees are off the clock. You will need to get their agreement to this first, but if you offer nice enough events, they may even look forward to it.

My team, with their newly hired manager, recently enjoyed a fun outing to our local major league baseball park to watch our hometown team play. Eating, drinking, dancing, singing, and cheering together was a bonding experience!

To Kevin and me, it was well worth the cost of the tickets, and no one on the staff complained that they didn't get paid for their time.

Other events that have worked well for my team are ice skating, bowling, outdoor picnics, walks that include a café visit, and nice holiday dinners at scenic restaurants. You will find your own event style based on your team surveys.

The purpose of hosting these events is to bring everyone on the team closer so that they communicate and collaborate more effectively. It can help renew your staff's spirits. It also benefits the job—not all companies will invest in teams like this, and individuals appreciate it and create valuable memories at these events.

Like hosting team-building activities, you want to host these events flawlessly. Do plenty of preparation ahead of time, keep the staff filled in on the details, double-check any reservations, and pull off the event smoothly.

❧ Travel Guides and Maps: Team Bonding ❧

The first time I ever heard of the concept of "team bonding" was from a woman named Olivia, a tall, pale brunette with quiet but intense energy. Olivia loves to travel more than anything else in the world.

At the young age of 19, she began a travel business while taking business courses at a local community college. Her travel enterprise was based on the premise that locals make the best travel guides. She tapped the people in various destinations who knew that area best and then produced travel guides that included hiking trails, restaurants, clubs, spas, and events like festivals and foot races.

Her success was surprisingly quick, and she began making money that she reinvested into the business. She left college and never went back.

Olivia's staff grew steadily until she employed ten travel agents. Then she expanded her business into new products like audio walking tours, books, maps with historical data, and the newest innovation in the travel industry: augmented reality, which ensures you can never be lost or bored in the travel spot of your choice anywhere in the world.

The travel agents she employed, a mix of men and women, got along fairly well, but Olivia always felt they could be closer and work better together. She considered trying to put on some team-building events herself, but when she discussed this with her staff, she got some serious eye rolls.

Her team was very clear that no one wanted to do the "trust fall" or participate in group hugs.

Not willing to give up, Olivia researched the subject and found a company in her city that puts on team-building events. This company, called "Feet First Eventertainment," has interesting approaches to creating more trust and loyalty among staff, so Olivia signed up.

The first event Olivia chose was the one called "Mission Possible," a scavenger hunt with a spy theme. Each team gets a packet of clues and attempts to solve puzzles while taking "undercover surveillance footage" around a designated area like a hotel, a theme park, or a city center. The event culminates at a restaurant where the organizers play the videos, revealing the winning team. The winning team gets a Spy Training Certificate.

It worked! Olivia's team jumped in and loved it.

Over the past few years, Olivia has continued to grow her business and participate in professionally staged team-building events with her team. She says she thinks investing in this is some of the best money she has ever spent on her business.

Key Takeaways

- Build close, functional team connections fostering a culture of trust, respect, and loyalty.

- Use team activities and events to promote better communication and collaboration among team members.

- Plan these events and activities regularly and with great care.

Part VII. The Amethyst Team: Advanced Training and Coaching

"Excellence is the gradual result of always striving to do better."

❧Pat Riley, former NBA head coach and three-time NBA Coach of the Year☙

The team was humming along at this point. Our new manager fit in, and everyone was getting along, working as a cohesive group, and enjoying the newly remodeled workspace. The customers (patients) were happy, and I felt like my color-coded, step-by-step management system was proving its effectiveness.

But some staff were younger team members without a ton of experience. No matter how much the employees liked each other, some weren't highly skilled at their jobs yet or skilled at collaborating in the way I would have wanted to see. On top of that, I needed to introduce more advanced topics like highly professional sales practices.

At the Powder Blue level, each staff member received his or her official job description, and Kevin trained them on each item, but that training was at a basic level. It was time to reach new heights. Kevin and I had to bring our A-game to coach each staff member. At the same time, we looked for inefficiencies to eliminate, sales scripts to refine, organizational opportunities to usher in, and techniques to hone. At this point, it was about performance.

We still had more to learn about our new team. Was each team member open to refining how he or she does things? Will the staff maintain a good attitude while being re-trained? Will they carry out all aspects of their job description with expertise?

I was committed to bringing the team's job performance up to astonishing heights. Not perfect, but definitely excellent. I had high hopes of finally transforming this group into an Indigo team.

Chapter 13. Advanced Training and Coaching

I define the difference between training and coaching: training is for teaching an employee *how* to do her job, and coaching is teaching her *how to do it better.*

High-value training will automatically lead to higher production and performance from your team. Plus, more advanced training gives the employee a greater understanding of responsibilities and, thus, builds confidence. This confidence will likely enhance overall performance, benefiting your company. Competent employees who stay on top of changing industry standards can help you become a market leader and a fierce competitor.

Investing in training shows your team that you value them and want to build them up. Team members will feel appreciated and more capable of performing, leading to increased morale and motivation.

How to Train New Employees Effectively

I encourage all my team members to take direction with a positive attitude as we train them (and later coach them) on their job duties. Emphasizing this point at staff meetings helps the employees understand that training and coaching will be ongoing in our company forever and will advance their careers as they learn to execute their responsibilities over time.

Any education, instruction, or tutoring is respectful so that it is a growing experience. If anyone feels criticized, judged, or put down by this instruction, he or she needs to let me, the owner, know immediately. That conversation must happen.

So often, people's early conditioning leads them to be defensive, and their ego gets riled up if anyone questions how they do things. A staff member, of course, is allowed to disagree with us on how to approach an issue or to ask why we want something a certain way, and we will answer questions, take feedback, and listen. But if we decide we want to make a change anyway, I need team members to be accommodating of our requests.

The best teams aren't formed overnight. It takes time to

train and coach them until they reach that Indigo level we've been aiming for since the start of this journey.

Let's take it one step at a time. This is a more detailed plan for training than we covered in the Powder Blue level since the complexity of the task has increased. Forming the Amethyst team is the final stage of the process before becoming Indigo.

Create a Plan Covering the Basics

Choose the best trainer for the job

Who is going to train which employee? Can you, as the owner, deliver the training, or is it best to delegate training to a close associate or an experienced employee? Coordinate the training program with whomever you think would be most effective for each staff member. The same person doesn't have to train all the employees; choose the best trainer for each person.

Allocate resources (supplies and time)

How will you find time to make this training happen? It sure is challenging to train employees during a bustling workday. The best way to handle this is to close the office for a full day, or even a half day, so everyone can focus on training. Just make sure you have an adequate amount of time to meet your instructional plan.

When your scheduled training time arrives, ensure your curriculum is well-prepared and that you have adequate tools to teach procedures and practices. Resources may include educational videos, software demonstrations, tools of the trade, or even outside help to assist with the process. This level of attention to detail can make or break your training program.

Develop a curriculum

Once you have researched, planned, and gathered all the necessary resources, it's time to focus on the training. Create training checklists so that you won't forget anything.

What is the schedule for your trainees? What tasks will you ask them to complete? How will you upgrade their skills? Identify the activities needed to accomplish your training goals.

Each team member already has a clearly defined job description and has had basic training at the Powder Blue level. It is time to revisit those job descriptions and refine and document the training instructions.

Does the employee have all the correct contact information for the vendors she needs? Can she find all the usernames and passwords necessary to accomplish the tasks assigned to her? Go over every line item on the job description with a high level of detail, update training materials as required, and ensure the employee has clarity and confidence regarding each task.

A test, a quiz, or a demonstration by the employee is an excellent last step to ensure the training is effective. As you plan your curriculum, plan this step as well. This step may solidify the employees' knowledge and give them (and you) confidence that a task has been mastered.

Train for Company Culture, Not Just Topics

Azure and Cobalt levels were about workplace culture. And Powder Blue begins with the company mission. Now that you have spent so much time understanding how to create excellent values and developing an inspiring mission statement, it's time to have your team internalize them. So, instead of merely focusing on practical information while training, take the time to talk about your company's priorities—fairness, kindness, integrity, and your other chosen values, while simultaneously emphasizing your mission.

Make regular adjustments to your training program

Finally, one of the best practices for employee training is demonstrating a continued commitment to your team's growth. Many employees take nearly six months, if not more, to settle into a company. They may not feel comfortable coming to you with their questions at first, so you must take extra measures to interact one-on-one with them.

Whether you schedule weekly or monthly staff meetings or in-person check-ins, the point is to stay close to your team. Otherwise, you risk cultivating an environment of complacency. Be willing to adjust your training program as needed and continue to evolve to keep up with employee needs and industry developments.

Training strategies for your Amethyst team

Here are some strategies that helped us the most when, at the Amethyst level, we trained our up-and-coming Indigo team.

Keeping notes during normal business operations

During regular days at the office, I sometimes noticed an employee struggling with something, or an unresolved issue would reveal itself. I knew it was likely that I would forget these minor conflicts or challenges (that later can turn into gigantic monsters) if I didn't note them down. So, I started the habit of keeping notes as I observed our team during regular working hours.

Since I always have my phone with me (as I'm sure you do), I write a small note to remind myself of something a team member said or did that I might want to address. I can't tell you how beneficial these notes have proven to be. You never want to attempt training or coaching when the business day is "live." Corrections and refinements must be saved for a more appropriate time, like at a staff meeting, a daily morning huddle (another Turquoise level communication tool), or a scheduled training day.

Life doesn't always work the way we want. You may devise the perfect training program, create an excellent schedule, and use all your resources, but there will remain gaps in your team's knowledge and skills. While some of these will only improve with time, others you can efficiently resolve if you're aware. So, every time you notice such a gap, write it down to remember to handle it later.

Covering areas for improvement at staff meetings

At your regularly scheduled staff meetings (established at

the Turquoise level), discuss any areas of improvement *for the whole team.* For example, if everyone in the office answers the phone, and you hear variations of how that is done, you could go over exactly how you would like the phone answered. Instead of singling out an employee you heard using a less-than-great greeting, you can talk to the team as one unit and encourage them to help each other out. Even if only one person needs extra help, talking about it to everyone can bring awareness, which means the entire team can resolve the issue.

Kevin and I started including simple group training in our monthly staff meetings, which helped us create more mutual understanding and interactions among our team. Eventually, it led to an improvement in the team's overall performance, which delighted us! But there are those situations when you want to train your employees in a one-on-one setting or include only the team members who need specific training. It can be boring for a person to be in training on a task they already know and perform well.

Scheduling extra training sessions as needed

As you recognize any training gaps or coaching needs that are more complicated, you can schedule extra workshops or training sessions by closing the office for a day or even just a couple of hours. It isn't necessary (or even possible) to train people only once and expect everything to be okay. As your business and industry evolve, you'll want to adjust and develop your education plan for the team. There will always be new tasks to learn and improvements to be made.

Sometimes, the market introduces new tools or methods that your competitors will start using, and you'll need to get on that train as quickly as you can. Upgrade your training program regularly and keep your team competent and polished!

Cultivate a positive attitude

Finally, when your staff needs corrections, training, and coaching, remember to view this as a favorable situation and a great opportunity. I've met managers who find it annoying when employees need to be guided or corrected. These managers believe you should be able to train someone once and that the employee should then do it correctly forever. That's the worst attitude to have toward your team! Refining each team member's skill level is an ongoing requirement to achieve an Indigo team.

Creating an Amethyst team is all about embracing changes and learning from mistakes. It's about constantly improving and inspiring others to do the same. You can't expect to survive in the professional world and stay ahead of the competition if you don't consistently upgrade your hired talent. Cultivating a positive attitude about training is crucial. It is your responsibility to ensure your team feels comfortable taking accountability for errors *and* being willing to improve.

As you do this, you'll create a group of people so dedicated to being better that there will be no room for failure or underperformance! And this is how we surround ourselves with higher vibrations as we move toward our final stage of team building.

❧*Surf's Up!*❧

I went to high school with adorable twin surfers, Noah and James Wilson. They had golden tans, friendly personalities, and a passion for food, cooking, and eating outdoors. The Wilson twins were known for having the best food on the beach *and* winning all the surf contests.

After graduation, I heard they had started a food truck business.

One day I went to the horse races and was happy to see a food truck festival at the track after the last race. I looked around for the Wilson twins, hoping to see them and reconnect.

And there they were. A food truck painted in bright colors depicting a local, vivid beach scene. The sign in front: "Surf's Up Beach Shack." The menu of smoothies, salads, tacos, and chili was written on an 11-foot surfboard leaning against the truck. About a dozen people were in line to order, and even more were waiting for their food. What better music than the Beach Boys to add to the fun?

I spotted Noah as he spoke to some customers for a few minutes before dashing back into the truck. I didn't get to speak to either of my friends that day as they were too busy feeding a crowd. But I was curious about how they put together their business in such a short amount of time.

Then, one morning, I ran into Noah at a local café. I told him I had seen his food truck at the horse track and asked him how he had launched his business. He said the most significant decision that he and his brother had made was realizing that, no matter how much they loved to cook, they couldn't run the business properly *and* do all the food production. The twins decided to hire chefs with the most potential and coach them.

Noah and James developed a comprehensive training program. They put months of work into training their chefs. Noah rented a commercial kitchen and conducted basic and advanced training classes. James observed and assisted with the lessons and had to make hiring changes based on how the chefs performed throughout the curriculum.

Noah said they figured if they got the food right, they would get the business right. They didn't want to lose control over the food quality, yet their training program could still yield the quality and variety they desired without the twins chopping every last onion.

Growing up with the twins, I always knew they were extraordinary cooks. But it turns out they are also great trainers of cooks! The twins have moved on to new ventures, which I imagine will be just as successful as their legendary food truck business.

Key Takeaways

- Encourage your staff to be open and positive about coaching on their job skills, work habits, and attitudes.

- Create a coherent plan for your advanced training program, and remember to focus on your mission and core values.

- Make a training checklist and be willing to adjust your plan as needed.

- Use creative methods to train your new hires and keep them engaged throughout the process.

- Observe training gaps during average days and schedule staff meetings or extra training sessions for the entire team.

Part VIII. Indigo Team: High Vibrations

> "Be the most passionate person in the room. Your energy
> and vibe will lift others as well."
>
> ❧Hiral Nagda☙

As Kevin and I reached this final stage of our team-building process, we noticed a complete shift in the energy around us. The office vibrations were higher than they had ever been. It was palpable.

At our optometry clinic, everyone suddenly seemed focused, involved, and energized once we reached the Amethyst level. I realized that we were close to creating a solid Indigo team! From Powder Blue forward, we had climbed the ladder and were finally positioned to reap the benefits of our hard work. I started to believe that we were close to having an Indigo team when I saw with my own eyes that the staff had integrated all the different color-coded levels into their daily work and were achieving outstanding results.

I knew they had learned about collaboration, but when

Shauna was out sick for a couple of days, Jennifer had to cover for her. Jennifer rose to the occasion and did a fabulous job. When Shauna returned to work, she bought Jennifer her favorite enormous latté drink. Jennifer seemed quite pleased with that, and when I asked her how she was feeling about doing all the work for a couple of days, she said she didn't mind because she knew Shauna would do the same thing for her whenever she needed it. Eureka! No resentment, bitterness, rudeness, or drama. Just teamwork on display.

This team worked harmoniously for five more years, accomplishing goals we previously thought impossible. Two of our team members became good friends, and their children played together. All of our team members treated each other with thoughtfulness and respect. We witnessed them enjoying their work, surroundings, the patients, and each other. It was a thing of beauty.

This Indigo team environment was what Kevin and I had always wanted to walk into every morning and what we wanted our staff, customers, and vendors to experience.

But how would we keep the vibes high and the money pouring into our business? We discovered if we paid attention to the *entire* color-coded system in a non-stop loop, things continued to get better! It was reminiscent of

how the Golden Gate bridge in San Francisco was painted:
by the time the crew finished painting the entire bridge,
it needed to be repainted, so they returned to the start and
initiated the process again.

Now that you have also developed an Amethyst team,
you should feel proud because it is no small feat. Each
team member has been trained, coached, mentored, and
encouraged to improve as he or she executes well-defined
job descriptions. But where do you go from here?

This team level is all about the "vibe" of the office and
how much it matters. As the owner (or manager of a team
within an organization), you have a great deal of control
over the mood and energy of the environment—more than
you might realize. That gives you the power to shift and
mold the feeling in your office. You want your demeanor,
behavior, and attitude to create a happy, harmonious, and
functional environment while discouraging negativity.

The Indigo team is focused on high energy and positivity.
This doesn't mean you ignore negative situations or
negative feelings. It means that once you have dealt with
these occurrences, you turn the focus back to everything
that is going well. It is your job (as the owner or manager
of your business) to pave the way to a high-energy, happy,

positive environment. You will know how to encourage a workplace with zeal and confidence and keep it that way.

But first, you must understand what a high vibration is. "High vibrational energy is a good and strong energy," says Marlene Vargas, co-founder of the metaphysical shop House of Intuition. The fantastic thing is that once energy and attitudes are high, staying there becomes a team habit. Yes, downfalls will occur, and anyone can have an off day, but once you've established a steady workflow and rhythm for your team, the system you have built will support you. Your office will continue to run smoothly and consistently. The secret to keeping it that way is to upgrade your systems, along with everyone's attitudes, regularly.

Chapter 14. Moods Are Contagious

Did you know that if you come to work in a sour mood, others in your space can easily "catch" your emotions? Scientific research has proven this, but it surprised Kevin and me. Even more surprising is that the prevailing mood in the office will affect achieving business goals.

Starting and running a business can be challenging, frustrating, and stressful. We thought we could hide our feelings so that none of the staff, customers, or vendors would know we were struggling. We just wouldn't talk about our feelings, we thought. Well, guess what? The energy that we bring through the front door is felt by everyone else, no matter how much we try to cover it. The scientific evidence is compelling that our emotions are as contagious as a cold or the flu. They spread freely to others in an organization.

Once we figured this out, we made a significant effort to deal with our attitudes and moods before coming to work (I'll explain below practical ways to do this). But then we also wanted our employees to do the same.

However, most people believe that employees are simply required to perform their job well and not make any big mistakes. Some might say, "It's not my boss' business whether I am cheerful and energetic or lethargic and sullen, as long as I perform my duties well." People often feel their emotions are locked inside and are no one else's concern.

While it is true that job performance is essential, there is a convincing body of research to show the ways a person's mood impacts those around him or her. In a 2009 study by Fowler and Christakis, researchers examined the impact of a person's emotions on his or her friends. They built a social network by connecting one friend to another friend and then measured the happiness or sadness of each person in the network. They found that:

- If you have a happy friend, the probability that you will be happier goes up by 25%; and

- Happy friends cluster together, and sad friends cluster together.

This principle works the same in a business office. The problem with employees lacking energy and enthusiasm is that their mood impacts others. They can pick others up or bring them down. Most people with a cold or flu bug work hard not to spread germs or infect others. But moods, believe it or not, are even more infectious than germs! My own experience has proven this to be true.

Why Raise Your Vibration?

Why am I writing about attaining a higher vibration? Why is it essential, other than it creates a more positive office environment? How does it lead to the highly profitable, harmonious, and efficient Indigo team?

Every one of us vibrates energetically at a particular frequency. The lower the frequency, the denser our energy and the more complex our problems seem. Here we may feel pain and discomfort in our physical body and experience emotions like anger, jealousy, sadness, and mental confusion. Psychically, our energy is darker. You must exert great effort to accomplish your goals in a low-vibration state. Your life takes on a negative quality because your feelings create your outer experience.

You can spot people like this because they love to talk about their problems, illnesses, and mental distress ("Ugh, the in-laws are visiting over the holidays, they are driving me crazy, I can't wait until they leave," etc.).

The higher your energy or vibration frequency, the lighter you feel in your physical, emotional, and mental bodies. You experience greater personal power, clarity, peace, love, and joy. You have little discomfort or pain in your physical body. Your energy is full of light! Your life flows with synchronicity, and you quickly manifest what you desire. Overall, your life takes on a positive quality which manifests in many smiles, laughter, and elevated conversations. Can you see how this will lead directly to accomplishing your team goals?

Raising your vibration will give your team and your business the best chance for success.

❧ The Impact of the Boss' Mood ❧

Joan, an ambitious and fiery thirty-something, had a middle-management position with great pay and benefits after 15 years in a major oil corporation. She felt like her career was on track *until* she received a promotion. This new position resulted in her being transferred to a new department, and she found herself with a curmudgeon of a boss named Henry.

Henry, an older, poorly groomed hulk of a man, was o.k. in the morning. He could even be charming. But after lunch, his personality would become sour, angry, and even rude.

Joan's first decision was to not let her boss' foul moods affect her or her work. She was going to ignore his rude, demeaning comments and was determined to produce the quality work for which she was known.

When Joan talked to her friends about this situation, they encouraged her to rise above the negative environment Henry created and, above all, to not put her career at stake over one jerk of a boss. She told them it was challenging dealing with a cheery boss in the morning, only to find he had morphed into the creature from the black lagoon by 3 p.m. Everyone agreed it was his problem, not hers, and advised Joan to shake off whatever negativity Henry brought to her workday.

But after weeks of dealing with Henry's lousy temper, Joan felt she couldn't take it anymore. She asked to meet with him privately to see if she could persuade him to stop yelling at her.

Joan felt nervous and shaky as she entered his office for this discussion. She had picked the first thing in the morning for the meeting time to try to catch him in his best mood. She had prepared her talking points the night before and was ready to request that if he had any problems with her work, he would tell her in private instead of shouting at her in front of other employees.

Joan bravely began, "I wanted to let you know I am

affected by your daily moodiness. I am hoping we can talk about this."

Henry replied, "I know I am not the most positive, upbeat person. But I am just trying to do my job and meet departmental goals."

Joan said, "I understand the pressure you are under to accomplish our goals, but your short temper and quickness to criticize are affecting my performance."

She worked at keeping her voice calm. "And I feel like, for the sake of our team, it would benefit you and all of us if you would set a more upbeat tone. A happy staff is more productive," she continued. Her voice cracked, and her palms were drenched with sweat.

Henry retaliated, "If you would just do your job correctly, I wouldn't be in a bad mood."

She explained how it bothered her to be criticized in front of others, but he continued to be defensive and not hear her. She could tell she was getting nowhere and maybe even making the situation worse because now he knew how she felt, which could make her a target.

Joan ended the meeting, feeling certain that communicating with Henry was a waste of time.

She decided her first instinct was right and became determined to make herself immune to his negativity. The worse his behavior became, the more she insulated herself from the bad vibrations he put out.

Joan began to notice how Henry's difficult nature was also affecting her co-workers. So she started having lunch with them and creating strategies to protect themselves from the toxicity. This worked well! As a team, they came up with these strategies:

> Take a walk outside when he is bringing you down;

> Take some deep breaths, and never feed the fire by engaging with him when he is upset;

> Focus on solving the problem at hand, not on his tantrum; and

> When he is attacking, think of something entirely different, like a beautiful vacation spot you enjoy.

Over time the team supported each other in using these tactics, and it worked! Joan outlasted Henry. Several months after Joan joined his group, he was moved to a different department. The manager who took Henry's place was even-keeled, kind, and brilliant.

Joan could have let Henry derail her career, but instead, she rose above the situation, and with patience, the situation resolved itself, and she continues to this day to have an amazingly successful career in the oil industry.

Chapter 15. Practical Ways to Achieve High Vibrations

How to Raise Your Vibration

1. Meditation is the number one technique most often mentioned in creating more positive energy inside yourself. There are volumes and volumes of information about how to meditate, but to simplify, just make sure you are spending some quality alone time (15 to 20 minutes every day) where you sit comfortably, take some deep breaths and relax your body and your mind. There are no right or wrong ways here—it is just a pause in the action for your peace of mind and mental health.

2. The technique that works for me every time I am feeling low (remember, our feelings are an indicator of our vibration) is to take a walk in nature. Any amount of time you can set aside for your walk will benefit you. Walk someplace beautiful, like a quiet tree-lined street or a neighborhood park. It can make all the difference in lifting your mood. Something about getting outside for fresh air and movement works like magic. Feel the breeze, soak up a little

sunshine, and watch the clouds drift. Enjoy taking in the flowers, butterflies, and birds. Your walk will help you feel refreshed and ready to face challenges with a positive mindset.

3. Be consistent with an exercise program that you enjoy. It might be yoga or running or working out in a gym. Any workout that leaves you invigorated will do! Thirty minutes three days a week should do the trick of keeping your body fit, which keeps your energy elevated. Of course, longer workouts and more days each week can only add more benefits.

4. Eat healthily. The better you eat, the better you will feel. It is only common sense. If you have a cup of coffee and a Snickers bar for breakfast, your mood might be cranky by lunchtime because your blood sugar will hit rock bottom. If you have a bowl of oatmeal topped with blueberries, you will likely feel sharper and more exhilarated. Keep your nutrition a high priority and be willing to spend money on high-quality food. A healthy diet leads to high vibrations.

5. Achieve a work-life balance. You will never feel your best if you don't take the time to enjoy the activities you truly love. Spending time with

your family and friends, participating in your
favorite hobbies, taking a nap, getting a massage,
or playing with a pet can lead to a happier life
and a better vibration for you to bring to work.
As an entrepreneur, you will probably work long
hours and have your business on your mind, but
your mood can suffer without achieving a balance
between work and play.

There are many more ways to raise your vibration, but if
you consistently give these five practices your time and
effort, it will take you further on the path to creating your
Indigo team.

Here are pragmatic ways to increase positivity throughout
your office. They are simple but not always easy. This
endeavor takes commitment and focus.

The Power of Words

It may sound too simple at first, but it's the holy grail of
most of your relationships in life: your words. What comes
out of your mouth can determine what kind of person you
are, how you treat people, what you value, and what you
want to communicate to others. How you interact and
talk with your team will go a long way in creating the

atmosphere inside your company.

All words carry a form of energy. Positive comments will lead to an outflow of positive energy, but negative remarks will do the opposite.

Once you've gone through all the different team levels, it will come down to your mindset and spirit. *To become completely Indigo, you'll want to make the conscious choice to let go of preconceived notions, previously held judgments, negative emotions, and past resentments. It's time to turn over a new leaf, grow and transform, and let old patterns dissipate.*

With the Indigo team strategy, I am committed to equip you with a methodology that will allow you to keep your team and business afloat at the highest functioning level for as long as you are in business. And to do that, it's of the utmost importance that you start prioritizing the little things that don't seem to make a difference at first but can move mountains once they pile up.

So, you might have streamlined your operations, communications, and productions, but now it all comes down to the nitty-gritty. The language you use, the emotions you convey, the energy you bring, and your mindset will all work to inspire others.

Morning Openings and Evening Closings

How do you arrive at the office each morning? Do you walk in quickly, coffee mug in hand, looking down and grunting a barely audible "Good morning" while making a beeline for your office? Or do you stride in energetically with good posture, glancing at the staff, smiling, and offering a sincere "Good morning!" and linger with them for a minute? It may seem only slightly different, but it sets the tone for the rest of the day. If they see that you are happy and confident, chances are, they will feel that way, too.

The same principles apply as you wrap up the day and leave the office. Do you seem exhausted, depleted, and ready to get home immediately? Or are you exhilarated by the success of your day, taking time to recap for a minute with your staff, and wishing everybody a sincere thank you and good evening? Words and demeanor matter when it comes to building an Indigo team.

Never kid yourself; the staff will always be reading your body language, facial expressions, moods, and tone. It is a huge responsibility to bring your best to them every workday. You are the leader, no one else. You'll be amazed by how much influence you have on the atmosphere of the office every day.

Raise Your Emotional Intelligence

Emotional intelligence, which includes sensitivity and empathy, is a quality all modern managers want to increase. Emotional intelligence simply means being aware of and managing your own emotions, which helps make you more perceptive of the feelings of others. It also encompasses understanding your emotions' impact on yourself and those around you, as discussed above. Emotional intelligence significantly affects how you react internally and externally to situations and affects how you handle interpersonal relationships. The higher an individual's emotional intelligence quotient (EQ), the better he or she can communicate.

Companies committed to excellent communication with their staff enjoy greater productivity and higher profitability due to employee satisfaction and retention rates, as we determined at the Turquoise level. Your level of emotional intelligence makes a big difference in your personal and professional success. The most successful leaders have high emotional intelligence, and as a leader, you will want to do everything you can to raise yours.

Decades of research point to emotional intelligence as a critical factor that sets top-performing managers apart. Believe it or not, emotional intelligence can make all the difference between an engaged employee and one who is burned out, frustrated, and unmotivated. Managers must pick up on signs that an employee is pushing themselves too far, which can cause burnout, depression, anxiety, and disengagement (like poor attendance). Often, a high-EQ manager will pick up on signs of these conditions before the employee approaches them to discuss the situation.

If you can be sensitive to your own feelings, you will be able to be sensitive to your team's feelings. Is someone feeling anxious? Is someone bored and not challenged? Be tuned in to the feelings of the people around you and deal with the situation gracefully but head-on. Managers with low EQ scores rarely notice how others are feeling, and even if they do, they will avoid having important discussions about what is happening.

Ask each employee how he is feeling in your one-on-one meetings and assure him that you will do what it takes to improve the situation.

When your EQ is high, it is also easier to see the best in others. This leads you to naturally praise your team members when you see them performing in a way you like.

Praise is one of the most profound principles of human nature: our need for recognition is real. As American psychologist and philosopher William James stated, "The deepest principle of human nature is a craving to be appreciated."

Teach Your Team Members How to Raise Their EQs

Now that you have worked on yourself, it is time to spread the concept of emotional intelligence to your team members. You can share your own experience and beliefs about this subject. Some may be more resistant to this concept because of habits they have held on to for years. Others will understand right away.

This doesn't mean that everyone must be positive all the time. We want to confront real feelings about work when they arise, no matter if they are positive or negative. But in general, focusing on the sunny side of things when possible is very helpful in lifting up the whole team.

One of our opticians recently got married in Las Vegas. We were all excited for her and had to make sacrifices in her absence. Upon her return, Kevin said, "Congratulations,

Sally! How was the wedding?" Sally replied with such a negative diatribe about everything that went wrong with the event that she had Kevin backing up slowly toward his office to be able to end the conversation.

Sally didn't mean to bring Kevin down; she was just telling him about her experience. But we realized that we needed to coach the entire staff on how to get a positive vibe at the office and keep in mind how their words can affect others. We were all willing to work a little harder to cover for her during her nuptials week, but it was so disheartening to find out it wasn't for such a great cause. Think how she could have lifted us all if she had focused on the positive aspects of her wedding and brought the feelings of love and romance to the forefront instead of all the negative occurrences. The place to share those struggles is with your family, friends, therapist, or journal. Can you imagine if everybody brought all their woes to the office daily? The vibe would go lower and lower.

After this put a damper on the office environment, Kevin and I devised a plan to teach the idea of creating a positive workplace for the whole team. Our strategy was two-fold:

1. We laid the foundation of the principle that moods are contagious and that a positive environment leads to a much higher level of success; and

2. We began role-playing exercises where we would demonstrate the difference between spreading positivity and spreading negativity.

We included these strategies in our staff meetings and discussed and practiced them in our one-on-one meetings. The whole team picked up on these principles, some faster than others, and over time we managed to create a high-vibration, harmonious, happy, and efficient Indigo team!

❧*An Unlikely Indigo Team*❧

Kristin began her career as a hairstylist when she was 19 years old. She had no college degree or management experience, yet she became a salon owner ten years later. This pretty, petite woman has maintained the same all-woman staff of hairstylists and receptionists for over five years.

Being a client in her salon, I can tell her staff is happy and drama-free. When I asked her how she maintained such a functional staff, she said that her ten years of being an employee taught her what works and what doesn't when running a team.

Kristen grew up with a gregarious, socially confident, and

friendly dad. She feels this led to her ability to bring people together, create a pleasant, respectful culture, and set a high vibration.

Kristen is a prime example of someone who has high Emotional Intelligence, and this quality alone increases her chances of building a successful team. She says she is always willing to sacrifice some money to promote a harmonious work culture. She could hire more hairstylists and make more money, but at what cost to the culture with the waves that would create?

She describes herself as someone sensitive to a person's energy and vibration and strives to give each employee exactly what he or she needs (the Platinum Rule). She also practices the Golden Rule of treating her employees with respect and never asking her employees to do anything she wouldn't be willing to do. She places herself in the team more as an equal than an authoritarian figure.

In hiring practices, she looks for positive, independent people who don't need micro-managing. If, after a few months, she finds that a new hire is not a fit for the positive, non-toxic culture she is trying to create, she gently guides the employee on how to straighten out the problem. She said some could turn their attitude around, and some she has had to let go.

I think Kristin has mastered the art of the Indigo team by using her high emotional intelligence better than most corporate managers and entrepreneurs.

Chapter 16. Set and Achieve Team Goals

As Kevin and I saw that we had a system now to manage our staff, we became curious about what heights we might be able to reach. So, we set a goal that seemed rather difficult, but if we could accomplish the goal, our dreams for our business and the staff's dreams for their careers would come true.

We decided to set a $10,000-a-day gross revenue goal, or $50,000 per week ($200,000 a month). It seemed overly ambitious when we first established this goal—about 20% higher than our average gross revenue.

Once we set this goal, we would see an occasional $10,000 day happen. We cheered and celebrated those days with big smiles and high-fives. Then those big money days started happening more frequently. To keep this momentum going, all seven of us pulled together as a team by reviewing the fundamentals of the Powder Blue level, the culture of Azure, and the communications of Turquoise. We continued discussing the physical space to get it right at the Cornflower level.

The ball kept rolling at the Cobalt level by building more robust, positive feelings for each team member. The Amethyst level never stopped because everyone can always learn more and improve their skills.

Then it began to happen. Day after day, the revenue was falling right around $10,000. The team was happy, efficient, and engaged.

We, as a team, had a peak moment at our annual summer picnic this year. We feasted on each other's dishes, played the Human Knot game, sat at a lovely picnic table under a giant oak tree, and had a productive team meeting. At the end of the meeting, I noticed how much laughter, chatter, smiles, and good vibes we shared around the table. I broke out in goosebumps because I realized we had finally done it! Here was an Indigo team. It took some time to get to this place. We had to be patient, but my team management system eventually led us to achieve our financial goals! And you can achieve your financial goals, too, as you follow this Indigo team system.

⮞Seeing the Positive⮜

My college friend Sean and I have maintained our friendship for many years. I knew him before college—he was my first date when I was 16. On that date, he told me he would be a millionaire in a few years. I was impressed and asked, "Will you buy me a horse when that happens?" He said, "Yes." Sean not only became a millionaire, but he also became a multimillionaire many times over. (He still owes me a horse.)

Sean is the ultimate Indigo team manager, and he influenced me greatly in creating my management system.

One day he invited me to a "bring a friend to work" day. He had worked his way up from accountant to CEO of a large industrial hardware computer company. These computers could withstand locations like the end of a dock out in the Northern Sea during winter.

When I arrived, I noticed that Sean was very organized. He had a spacious, glossy, walnut desk; the only thing on it was a current project file.

He said, "Come on, let's go down to the basement and meet the guys."

When we entered the basement, his manufacturing team greeted him with enthusiasm, waving and smiling. I followed Sean around the immaculate production facility. He was friendly with each individual, inquiring about family and hobbies. It was clear he cared about them, and they cared about him.

I was surprised that a CEO met face-to-face regularly with his front-line production workers. I asked Sean if he had middle managers working for him. He said he did, and meeting with them regularly was important, too. But he liked to know all his staff and make it one big family.

After a little small talk, Sean and the factory workers talked shop. He asked questions, listening intently to their answers. After shaking hands, Sean patted each team member on the back and moved on to the next employee.

After we met everybody on the assembly line and returned to Sean's luxurious office, we discussed the employees I had just met, and he told me about their backgrounds. I noticed he did not say one negative thing about any of them!

Sean led this computer hardware business to the heights of success and earned around $10 million in stock options when the owners sold the company. It taught me that there is no limit to what a real Indigo team can accomplish.

Key Takeaways

- The energy people bring into the office is real and matters.

- Understand and teach your staff that moods are contagious.

- High energy, motivation, and positivity goals of the entire team.

- As the manager/owner, you are responsible for setting the tone for the entire office.

- Learn how to encourage and nurture a positive workplace environment.

- Raise your emotional intelligence; it will pay off!

- Your words and actions matter in achieving a high vibration throughout your business.

Conclusion. Now It's Your Turn

"True leadership is about striving to become better in all areas of life and empowering everyone around you to become the best versions of themselves."

&Brian Tracy&

With the Indigo team system, Kevin and I created a wonderful place to work. Of course, it was not just the two of us but also the entire team who participated in the turnaround. We were able to end the negativity, drama, and boredom that can spread through a group. Once we implemented this system, we experienced less turnover and fewer frustrating bad days. We gained confidence that we could create and run a team as well or better than any MBA.

You now have the keys to do this.

When you start your own business, or manage a team within an organization, you know that you are great at what you do. But that does not guarantee you will have the knowledge or natural ability to run a happy, harmonious, and efficient team, which is essential to making your work a huge success. This book is your road map to do just that!

Building an Indigo team has changed our lives and the lives of our team members, and I hope it changes yours for the better, too.

We started at Powder Blue and learned the importance of having a clear mission statement and clear job descriptions. Then, we moved on to Azure, where it was all about finding the right people for our team and sowing seeds for an effective and optimistic culture. Next, the Turquoise level was about building robust communication systems, and Cornflower focused on creating and optimizing a physical space for comfort and efficiency. After that came Cobalt— bonding to build a trustworthy, loyal, and respectful team. Then the Amethyst level guided us on advanced team training and coaching to hone our skills. Finally, we raised our level of positivity and energy to become purely Indigo!

With this color-coded, step-by-step system, you can manage and lead your team to heights you may not have imagined.

Frankly, our optometry office was a chaotic mess during its early years. Still, we learned from it and became eager to share our formula for success so that you could create and maintain your Indigo team.

Since we figured out and applied the Indigo team system, we have had many years of ease and profitability. Our staff members and patients have also significantly benefited from this system.

Start at the beginning by implementing Powder Blue level principles, and don't stop until your carefully chosen team is humming with energy, productivity, and positivity. You will know you have achieved the Indigo level when your bank account is healthy and your days at the office are a delight. Happy team building!

References

6 Easy Ways to Improve Your Workstation Ergonomics. (n.d.). www.labfurnishings.com. Retrieved June 1, 2021, from https://labfurnishing.com/6-easy-ways-to-improve-workstation-ergonomics

11 creative ways to improve team performance. (n.d.). www.project.co. Retrieved June 26, 2021, from https://www.project.co/improve-team-performance/

Arbeau, M. (2013, December 8). *The Energy of Words: Use the Vibration of Language to Manifest the Life You Desire.* www.scribd.com. Retrieved March 3, 2021, from https://www.scribd.com/book/274103530/The-Energy-of-Words-Use-the-Vibration-of-Language-to-Manifest-the-Life-You-Desire

Bachrach, A. (2021, August 11). *7 Steps to Effective Communication Skills that Get Results.* www.zenbusiness.com. Retrieved July 2, 2021, from https://www.zenbusiness.com/blog/effective-communication/

Belle, G. (2021, February 16). *7 Work Office Decorating Ideas To Inspire Creativity & Productivity.* www.glossybelle.com. Retrieved June 12, 2021, from https://

glossybelle.com/work-office-decorating-ideas-to-inspire-creativity-and-productivity/

Chowdhury, M. R. (2021, November 25). *How to Foster Compassion at Work Through Compassionate Leadership.* www.positivepsychology.com. Retrieved August 8, 2021, from https://positivepsychology.com/compassion-at-work-leadership/

Collins, J. (2001). *From Good to Great* (1st Edition). Harper Business.

Costa, D. (2019, April 10). *7 Steps to Making the Hiring Process Easier.* www.skeeled.com. Retrieved June 26, 2021, from https://www.skeeled.com/blog/7-steps-to-make-the-hiring-process-easier-and-faster

Covey, S. (Ed.). (2020). Habit #2 Begin with the End in Mind. In *The Seven Habits of Highly Effective People* (pp. 109–110). Simon & Schuster.

Cuncic, A. (2020, May 25). *How to Practice Active Listening.* www.verywellmind.com. Retrieved May 10, 2021, from https://www.verywellmind.com/what-is-active-listening-3024343

Fairness in the Workplace. (n.d.). www.staffscapes.com. Retrieved May 31, 2021, from https://staffscapes.com/fairness-in-the-workplace/#:

Folkman, J. (2014, April 2). *Mood And Engagement Are Contagious.* www.forbes.com. Retrieved July 30, 2021, from https://www.forbes.com/sites/joefolkman/2014/04/02/mood-and-engagement-are-contagious/?sh=2f463c135529

goFluent. (2017, May 23). *The Importance of Coaching in Training.* www.gofluent.com. Retrieved June 30, 2021, from https://www.gofluent.com/blog/importance-coaching-training/

Grossman, D. (2021, November 29). *Improve the Employer-Employee Connection with Communication.* www.yourthoughtpartner.com. Retrieved July 12, 2021, from https://www.yourthoughtpartner.com/blog/improve-the-employer-employee-connection-with-communication

Hearn, S. (2019, November 12). *Qualities of a Good Manager: 13 Soft Skills You Need.* www.fond.co. Retrieved April 21, 2021, from https://www.fond.co/blog/qualities-of-a-good-manager/

How the Big Five Personality Traits Influence Work Behavior. (n.d.). www.floridatechonline.com. Retrieved

July 18, 2021, from https://www.floridatechonline.com/
blog/business/how-the-big-five-personality-traits-influence-
work-behavior/

Kankousky, M. (n.d.). *Coaching employees: 5 steps to
making it more effective.* www.insperity.com. Retrieved
April 13, 2021, from https://www.insperity.com/blog/
coaching-employees/

Kappel, M. (2017, April 5). *5 Tips on How to Fire an
Employee Gracefully.* www.forbes.com. Retrieved
July 18, 2021, from https://www.forbes.com/sites/
mikekappel/2017/04/05/5-tips-on-how-to-fire-an-
employee-gracefully/?sh=8de52ab29dd5

Loosbrock, D. J. S. (2019, September 10). *4 Reasons Why
Every Manager Should Care About Emotional Intelligence.*
www.fond.co. Retrieved August 15, 2021, from https://
www.fond.co/blog/4-reasons-emotional-intelligence/

Lotich, P. (2019, January 9). *10 Qualities of a Great Boss.*
www.thethrivingsmallbusiness.com. Retrieved May 7,
2021, from https://thethrivingsmallbusiness.com/how-to-
be-a-great-boss/

McDaniel, M. A., Whetzel, D. L., Schmidt, F. L., &
Maurer, S. D. (1994). The validity of employment

interviews: A comprehensive review and meta-analysis. *Journal of Applied Psychology*, **79**(4), 599–616. https://doi. org/10.1037/0021-9010.79.4.599

Paige, A. (n.d.). *How to Do a Job Evaluation.* www. smallbusiness.chron.com. Retrieved June 7, 2021, from https://smallbusiness.chron.com/job-evaluation-2580.html

Pope, A. (n.d.). *31 Engaging Team Meeting Ideas and Activities to Start Your Day.* www.timedoctor.com. Retrieved August 1, 2021, from https://biz30.timedoctor. com/morning-meeting-activities/

Runtaugh, P. D. (2012, September 29). *The Benefits of Being in a Higher Vibration.* www.huffpost.com. Retrieved September 8, 2021, from https://www.huffpost.com/entry/ positive-energy_b_1715767

Shulman, A. (n.d.). *8 Tips for Better Vibes in Your Home & Workplace.* www.raiseyourvibrationtoday.com. Retrieved August 7, 2021, from https://raiseyourvibrationtoday.com/ uncategorized/add-positive-vibes-home-workspace/

Simons, R. (2016, August 25). *How to Avoid the Pain Associated with Firing an Employee.* www.recruiter.com. Retrieved August 1, 2021, from https://www.recruiter.

com/i/how-to-avoid-the-pain-associated-with-firing-an-employee/

Tannenbaum, S. I., Beard, R. L., & Salas, E. (1992). Team building and its influence on team effectiveness: An examination of conceptual and empirical developments. In K. Kelley (Ed.), *Issues, theory, and research in industrial/ organizational psychology* (pp. 117-153). Amsterdam: Elsevier. http://dx.doi.org/10.1016/S0166-4115(08)62601-1

The Comfy Team. (2016, May 10). *The Comfort Productivity Connection.* www.comfyapp.com. Retrieved June 7, 2021, from https://comfyapp.com/the-comfort-productivity-connection/

The Young Entrepreneur Council. (2021, June 16). *13 Best Practices for Building Solid Small Business Operations.* www.smallbiztrends.com. Retrieved April 10, 2021, from https://smallbiztrends.com/2014/06/best-practices-small-business-operations.html

About the Author

Valerie Riggs believes in the power of indigo. She's created a system of building blocks—from "powder blue" to "indigo"—that help build productive teams in any business setting.

Val comes from a corporate background. Working with American Airlines and Chevron Corporation, and later with Backroads Bicycle Touring, Val gained experience managing teams and, just as important, in all the ways *not* to manage a team.

When her husband needed help directing his optometry practice, Val jumped in to create a profitable and harmonious team by modifying corporate management methods and updating them for modern entrepreneurs.

Valerie has been a published writer since 1998, when she began writing a weekly column for tourists in her town's local newspaper, *The Del Mar Times*. Seal Press published her essay in the non-fiction book *Why We Ride*, edited by Verna Dreisbach.

Before her father passed away, Val and her father published a young adult historical novel, *Apache Pony Whisperer*, which tells the story of how the great Apache Indian Chief Geronimo's nephew—with his superb horse-training skills—helps his tribe win battles during the Apache Wars.

Val was born and raised in San Diego, California, and still resides in her beloved hometown.

Made in United States
Troutdale, OR
03/12/2024

18383195R00126